by Tom Stoppard

ROSENCRANTZ AND GUILDENSTERN ARE DEAD

THE REAL INSPECTOR HOUND

ENTER A FREE MAN

AFTER MAGRITTE

JUMPERS

TRAVESTIES

DIRTY LINEN AND NEW-FOUND-LAND

EVERY GOOD BOY DESERVES FAVOUR
and PROFESSIONAL FOUL

NIGHT AND DAY

DOGG'S HAMLET, CAHOOT'S MACBETH

ON THE RAZZLE
(*adapted from Johann Nestroy's*
Einen Jux will er sich machen)

THE REAL THING
THE DOG IT WAS THAT DIED AND OTHER PLAYS

SQUARING THE CIRCLE
with EVERY GOOD BOY DESERVES FAVOUR
and PROFESSIONAL FOUL

FOUR PLAYS FOR RADIO: ARTIST DESCENDING A STAIRCASE,
WHERE ARE THEY NOW?, IF YOU'RE GLAD I'LL BE FRANK
and ALBERT'S BRIDGE

HAPGOOD

and a novel

LORD MALQUIST AND MR MOON

ROUGH CROSSING
(*adapted from Ferenc Molnár's* Play at the Castle)

DALLIANCE
and UNDISCOVERED COUNTRY
(*a version of Arthur Schnitzler's* Das weite Land)

THE REAL THING

THE
REAL THING

TOM STOPPARD

faber and faber
LONDON · BOSTON

First published in 1982
by Faber and Faber Limited
3 Queen Square London WC1N 3AU
Reprinted with revisions 1983, 1984
Reprinted with further revisions 1986 and 1988
Reprinted 1989 and 1991

Printed in Great Britain by
Cox & Wyman Ltd, Reading, Berkshire
All rights reserved

© Tom Stoppard, 1982, 1983, 1986

A CIP record for this book
is available from the British Library

ISBN 0-571-11983-2 Pbk

For Miriam

CHARACTERS

MAX, 40-ish
CHARLOTTE, 35-ish
HENRY, 40-ish
ANNIE, 30-ish
BILLY, 22-ish
DEBBIE, 17
BRODIE, 25

The Real Thing opened on 16 November 1982
at the Strand Theatre, London
with the following cast:

MAX	Jeremy Clyde
CHARLOTTE	Polly Adams
HENRY	Roger Rees
ANNIE	Felicity Kendal
BILLY	Michael Thomas
DEBBIE	Susanna Hamilton
BRODIE	Ian Oliver

Directed by Peter Wood
Lighting by William Bundy
Designed by Carl Toms
Presented by Michael Codron

ACT ONE

SCENE ONE

MAX *and* CHARLOTTE.

MAX *doesn't have to be physically impressive, but you wouldn't want him for an enemy.* CHARLOTTE *doesn't have to be especially attractive, but you instantly want her for a friend.*

Living-room. Architect's drawing board, perhaps. A partly open door leads to an unseen hall and an unseen front door. One or two other doors to other rooms.

MAX *is alone, sitting in a comfortable chair, with a glass of wine and an open bottle to hand. He is using a pack of playing cards to build a pyramidical, tiered viaduct on the coffee table in front of him. He is about to add a pair of playing cards (leaning against each other to hold each other up), and the pyramid is going well. Beyond the door to the hall, the front door is heard being opened with a key. The light from there changes as the unseen front door is opened.*

MAX *does not react to the opening of the door, which is more behind him than in front of him.*

MAX: Don't slam—
      (*The front door slams, not violently. The viaduct of cards collapses.*)
      (*Superfluously, philosophically*) . . . the door.
      (CHARLOTTE, *in the hall, wearing a topcoat, looks round the door just long enough to say two words and disappears again.*)
CHARLOTTE: It's me.
      (MAX *leaves the cards where they have fallen. He takes a drink from the glass. He doesn't look up at all.*
      CHARLOTTE, *without the topcoat, comes back into the room carrying a small suitcase and a plastic duty-free airport bag.*

9

She puts the case down and comes up behind MAX's *chair and kisses the top of his head.*)

CHARLOTTE: Hello.

MAX: Hello, lover.

CHARLOTTE: That's nice. You used to call me lover.

(*She drops the airport bag on his lap and returns towards the suitcase.*)

MAX: Oh, it's you. I thought it was my lover. (*He doesn't look at his present. He puts the bag on the floor by his chair.*) Where is it you've been?

(*The question surprises her. She is deflected from picking up her suitcase—presumably to take it into the bedroom—and the case remains where it is.*)

CHARLOTTE: Well, Switzerland, of course. Weren't you listening?

(MAX *finally looks at her.*)

MAX: You look well. Done you good.

CHARLOTTE: What, since yesterday?

MAX: Well, something has. How's Ba'l?

CHARLOTTE: Who?

(MAX *affects to puzzle very briefly over her answer.*)

MAX: I meant Ba'l.

Do you say 'Basel'?

I say Ba'l.

CHARLOTTE: Oh . . . yes. I say Basel.

MAX: (*Lilts*) 'Let's call the whole thing *off* . . .'

(CHARLOTTE *studies him briefly, quizzically.*)

CHARLOTTE: Fancy a drink?

(*She notes the glass, the bottle and his behaviour.*)

(*Pointedly, but affectionately*) Another drink?

(*He smiles at her, empties his glass and holds it up for her. She takes the glass, finds a second glass, pours wine into both glasses and gives* MAX *his own glass.*)

MAX: How's old Basel, then? Keeping fit?

CHARLOTTE: Are you a tiny bit sloshed?

MAX: Certainly.

CHARLOTTE: I didn't go to Basel.

(MAX *is discreetly but definitely interested by that.*)

MAX: No? Where did you go, then?

CHARLOTTE: Geneva.

    (MAX *is surprised. He cackles.*)

MAX: Geneva!

    (*He drinks from his glass.*)

    How's old Geneva, then? Franc doing well?

CHARLOTTE: Who?

    (*He affects surprise.*)

MAX: The Swiss franc. Is it doing well?

CHARLOTTE: Are you all right?

MAX: Absolutely.

CHARLOTTE: How have you got on?

MAX: Not bad. My best was eleven pairs on the bottom row, but
    I ran out of cards.

CHARLOTTE: What about the thing you were working on? . . .
    What is it?

MAX: An hotel.

CHARLOTTE: Yes. You were two elevators short.

MAX: I've cracked it.

CHARLOTTE: Good.

MAX: I'm turning the whole place on its side and making it a
    bungalow. I still have a problem with the rooftop pool. As
    far as I can see, all the water is going to fall into the shallow
    end. How's the lake, by the way?

CHARLOTTE: What lake?

    (*He affects surprise.*)

MAX: Lake Geneva. You haven't been to Virginia Water, have
    you? Lake Geneva. It is at Geneva? It must be. They
    wouldn't call it Lake Geneva if it was at Ba'l or Basel.
    They'd call it Lake Ba'l or Basel. You know the Swiss.
    Utterly reliable. And they've done it without going digital,
    that's what I admire so much. They know it's all a snare and
    a delusion. I can remember digitals when they first came out.
    You had to give your wrist a vigorous shake like bringing
    down a thermometer, and the only place you could buy one
    was Tokyo. But it looked all over for the fifteen-jewelled
    movement. Men ran through the market place shouting, 'The
    cog is dead.' But still the Swiss didn't panic. In fact, they
    made a few digitals themselves, as a feint to draw the

11

Japanese further into the mire, and got on with numbering the bank accounts. And now you see how the Japs are desperately putting hands on their digital watches. It's yodelling in the dark. They can yodel till the cows come home. The days of the digitals are numbered. The metaphor is built into them like a self-destruct mechanism. Mark my words, I was right about the skate-board, I was right about *nouvelle cuisine*, and I'll be proved right about the digital watch. Digitals have got no class, you see. They're science and technology. Makes nonsense of a decent pair of cufflinks, as the Swiss are the first to understand. Good sale?

(CHARLOTTE *stares at him.*)

CHARLOTTE: What?

(*He affects surprise.*)

MAX: Good sale. Was the sale good? The sale in Geneva, how was it? Did it go well in Geneva, the sale?

CHARLOTTE: What's the matter?

MAX: I'm showing an interest in your work. I thought you liked me showing an interest in your work. *My* showing. Save the gerund and screw the whale. Yes, I'm sure you do. I remember how cross you got when I said to someone, 'My wife works for Sotheby's or Christie's, I forget which.' You misjudged me, as it happens. You thought I was being smart at your expense. In fact, I had forgotten. How's old Christie, by the way? (*Strikes his forehead.*) There I go. How's old Sothers, by the way? Happy with the Geneva sale, I trust?

(CHARLOTTE *puts her glass down and moves to stand facing him.*)

CHARLOTTE: (*To call a halt*) All right.

MAX: Just all right? Well, that's the bloody Swiss for you. Conservative, you see. The Japs could show them a thing or two. They'd have a whaling fleet in Lake Geneva by now. How's the skiing, by the way? Plenty of snow?

CHARLOTTE: Stop it—stop it—*stop it.*
    What have I done?

MAX: You forgot your passport.

CHARLOTTE: I did what?

MAX: You went to Switzerland without your passport.

12

CHARLOTTE: What makes you think that?

MAX: I found it in your recipe drawer.

CHARLOTTE: (*Quietly*) Jesus God.

MAX: Quite.

(CHARLOTTE *moves away and looks at him with some curiosity.*)

CHARLOTTE: What were you looking for?

MAX: Your passport.

CHARLOTTE: It's about the last place I would have looked.

MAX: It was.

CHARLOTTE: Why were you looking for it?

MAX: I didn't know it was going to be your passport. If you see what I mean.

CHARLOTTE: I think I do. You go through my things when I'm away? (*Pause. Puzzled.*) Why?

MAX: I liked it when I found nothing. You should have just put it in your handbag. We'd still be an ideal couple. So to speak.

CHARLOTTE: Wouldn't you have checked to see if it had been stamped?

MAX: That's a very good point. I notice that you never went to Amsterdam when you went to Amsterdam. I must say I take my hat off to you, coming home with Rembrandt place mats for your mother. It's those little touches that lift adultery out of the moral arena and make it a matter of style.

CHARLOTTE: I wouldn't go on, if I were you.

MAX: Rembrandt place mats! I wonder who's got the originals. Some Arab, is it? 'Put the Rembrandts round, Abdul, and tell the kids to wash their hands, it's shoulder of goat.'

CHARLOTTE: It's like when we were burgled. The same violation. Worse.

MAX: I'm not a burglar. I'm your husband.

CHARLOTTE: As I said. Worse.

MAX: Well, I'm sorry.

I think I just apologized for finding out that you've deceived me.

Yes, I did.

13

How does she do it?

(*She moves away, to leave the room.*)

Are you going somewhere?

CHARLOTTE: I'm going to bed.

MAX: Aren't you going to tell me who it is?

CHARLOTTE: Who what is?

MAX: Your lover, lover.

CHARLOTTE: Which lover?

MAX: I assumed there'd only be the one.

CHARLOTTE: Did you?

MAX: Well, do you see them separately or both together?
Sorry, that's not fair.
Well, tell you what, nod your head if it's separately.

(*She looks at him.*)

Heavens.
If you have an opening free, I'm not doing much at the moment. Or is the position taken?
It is only two, is it?
Nod your head.

(*She looks at him.*)

Golly, you are a dark horse. How do they all three get away at the same time? Do they work together, like the Marx Brothers?
I'm not upsetting you, I hope?

CHARLOTTE: You underestimate me.

MAX: (*Interested*) Do I? A string quartet, you mean? That sort of thing?

(*He ponders for a moment.*)

What does the fourth one do?

(*She raises her hand.*)

Got it. Plays by himself.
You can slap me if you like. I won't slap you back. I abhor cliché. It's one of the things that has kept me faithful.

(CHARLOTTE *returns to the hall and reappears wearing her topcoat.*)

CHARLOTTE: If you don't mind, I think I will go out after all.

(*She moves to close the door behind her.*)

MAX: You've forgotten your suitcase.

(Pause. She comes back and picks up the suitcase. She takes the case to the door.)

CHARLOTTE: I'm sorry if you've had a bad time. But you've done everything wrong. There's a right thing to say if you can think what it is.

(She waits a moment while MAX thinks.)

MAX: Is it anyone I know?

CHARLOTTE: You aren't anyone I know.

(She goes out, closing the door, and then the front door is heard opening and closing.

MAX remains seated. After a moment he reaches down for the airport bag, puts it back on his lap and looks inside it. He starts to laugh. He withdraws from the bag a miniature Alp in a glass bowl. He gives the bowl a shake and creates a snowstorm within it. Then the snowstorm envelops the stage. Music—a pop record—makes a bridge into the next scene.)

SCENE TWO

HENRY, CHARLOTTE, MAX *and* ANNIE.

HENRY *is amiable but can take care of himself.* CHARLOTTE *is less amiable and can take even better care of herself.* MAX *is nice, seldom assertive, conciliatory.* ANNIE *is very much like the woman whom* CHARLOTTE *has ceased to be.*

A living-room. A record player and shelves of records. Sunday newspapers.

The music is coming from the record player.

HENRY, *with several record sleeves around him, is searching for a particular piece of music.*

There are doors to hall, kitchen, bedroom. CHARLOTTE *enters barefoot, wearing* HENRY'S *dressing-gown which is too big for her. She is unkempt from sleep and seems generally disordered.*

HENRY *looks up briefly.*

15

HENRY: Hello.

(CHARLOTTE *moves forward without answering, sits down and looks around in a hopeless way.*)

CHARLOTTE: Oh, God.

HENRY: I thought you'd rather lie in. Do you want some coffee?

CHARLOTTE: I don't know. (*Possibly referring to the litter of record sleeves, wanly.*) What a mess.

HENRY: Don't worry . . . don't worry . . .

(HENRY *continues to search among the records.*)

CHARLOTTE: I think I'll just stay in bed.

HENRY: Actually, I phoned Max.

CHARLOTTE: What? Why?

HENRY: He was on my conscience. He's coming round.

CHARLOTTE: (*Quite strongly*) I don't want to see *him*.

HENRY: Sorry.

CHARLOTTE: Honestly, Henry.

HENRY: Hang on—I think I've found it.

(*He removes the pop record, which might have come to its natural end by now, from the record player and puts a different record on. Meanwhile—*)

CHARLOTTE: Are you still doing your list?

HENRY: Mmm.

CHARLOTTE: Have you got a favourite book?

HENRY: *Finnegans Wake.*

CHARLOTTE: Have you read it?

HENRY: Don't be difficult.

(*He lowers the arm on to the record and listens to a few bars of alpine Strauss—or sub-Strauss. Then he lifts the arm again.*)

No . . . No . . . Damnation.

(*He starts to put the record away.*)

Do you remember when we were in some place like Bournemouth or Deauville, and there was an open-air dance floor right outside our window?

CHARLOTTE: No.

HENRY: Yes you do, I was writing my Sartre play, and there was this bloody orchestra which kept coming back to the same tune every twenty minutes, so I started shouting out of the window and the hotel manager—

CHARLOTTE: That was Zermatt. (*Scornfully*) *Bournemouth.*

HENRY: Well, what was it?

CHARLOTTE: What was what?

HENRY: What was the tune called? It sounded like Strauss or somebody.

CHARLOTTE: How does it go?

HENRY: I don't know, do I?

CHARLOTTE: Who were you with in Bournemouth?

HENRY: Don't mess about. I'm supposed to give them my eight records tomorrow, and so far I've got five and *Finnegans Wake.*

CHARLOTTE: Well, if you don't know what it's called and you can't remember how it goes, why in Christ's name do you want it on your desert island?

HENRY: It's not supposed to be eight records you love and adore.

CHARLOTTE: Yes, it is.

HENRY: It is not. It's supposed to be eight records you associate with turning-points in your life.

CHARLOTTE: Well, I'm a turning-point in your life, and when you took me to Zermatt your favourite record was the Ronettes doing 'Da Doo Ron Ron'.

HENRY: The Crystals. (*Scornfully*) The Ronettes.

(CHARLOTTE *gets up and during the following searches, successfully, for a record, which she ends up putting on the machine.*)

CHARLOTTE: You're going about this the wrong way. Just pick your eight all-time greats and then remember what you were doing at the time. What's wrong with that?

HENRY: I'm supposed to be one of your intellectual playwrights. I'm going to look a total prick, aren't I, announcing that while I was telling Jean-Paul Sartre and the post-war French existentialists where they had got it wrong, I was spending the whole time listening to the Crystals singing 'Da Doo Ron Ron'. Look, ages ago, Debbie put on one of those classical but not too classical records—she must have been about ten or eleven, it was before she dyed her hair— and I said to you, 'That's that bloody tune they were driving me mad with when I was trying to write "Jean-Paul

17

is up the Wall" in that hotel in Deauville all those years ago.' Or Zermatt. Maybe *she'll* remember.

CHARLOTTE: Where is she?

(CHARLOTTE *has placed the record on the machine, which now starts to play the Skater's Waltz.*)

HENRY: Riding stables.

That's it! (*Triumphant and pleased, examining the record sleeve.*) *Skater's Waltz!* How did you know?

CHARLOTTE: They don't have open-air dance floors in the Alps in mid-winter. They have skating rinks. Now you've got six.

HENRY: Oh, I can't use that. It's so banal.

(*The doorbell rings.* HENRY *goes to take the record off the machine.*)

That's Max. Do you want to let him in?

CHARLOTTE: No. Say I'm not here.

HENRY: He knows perfectly well you're here. Where else would you be? I'll say you don't want to see him because you've seen quite enough of him. How's that?

CHARLOTTE: (*Giving up*) Oh, I'll get dressed.

(*She goes out the way she came in, towards the bedroom.* HENRY *goes out through another door into the hall. His voice and* MAX's *voice are heard, and the two men come in immediately afterwards.*)

HENRY: Hello, Max. Come in.

MAX: Hello, Henry.

HENRY: (*Entering*) It's been some time.

(MAX *enters unassertively.*)

MAX: Well, you've rather been keeping out of the way, haven't you?

HENRY: Yes. I'm sorry, Max. (*Indicating the bedroom*) Charlotte's not here. How are you?

MAX: I'm all right.

HENRY: Good.

MAX: And you?

HENRY: I'm all right.

MAX: Good.

HENRY: Well, we all seem to be all right.

MAX: Is Charlotte all right?

18

HENRY: I don't think she's terribly happy. Well, is it coffee or open a bottle?

MAX: Bottle, I should think.

HENRY: Hang on, then.

(HENRY *goes out through the door to the kitchen.* MAX *turns aside and looks at a paper without interest.* CHARLOTTE *enters from the bedroom, having dressed without trying hard. She regards* MAX, *who then notices her.*)

MAX: Hello, darling.

CHARLOTTE: Don't I get a day off?

MAX: (*Apologetically*) Henry phoned . . .

CHARLOTTE: (*More kindly*) It's all right, Max.

(HENRY *enters busily from the kitchen, carrying an open champagne bottle and a jug of orange juice. Wine glasses are available in the living-room.* HENRY *puts himself in charge of arranging the drinks.*)

HENRY: Hello, Charlotte. I was just telling Max you weren't here. So nice to see you, Max. What are you doing with yourself?

MAX: Is he joking?

HENRY: I mean apart from that. Actors are so sensitive. They feel neglected if one isn't constantly checking up on them.

MAX: I was just telling Henry off for keeping out of the way.

CHARLOTTE: You'd keep out of the way if you'd written it. (*To* HENRY.) If that orange juice is for me, you can forget it.

HENRY: No, no—buck's fizz all round. I feel reckless, extravagant, famous, in love, and I'm next week's castaway on *Desert Island Discs*.

MAX: Are you really?

HENRY: Head over heels.

How was last night, by the way?

(*He hands* MAX *and* CHARLOTTE *their glasses.*)

CHARLOTTE: Hopeless. I had to fake it again.

HENRY: Very witty woman, my present wife. Actually, I was talking about my play.

CHARLOTTE: Actually, so was I. I've decided it's a mistake appearing in Henry's play.

MAX: Not for me, it isn't.

19

CHARLOTTE: Well, of course not for you, you idiot, you're not his wife.

MAX: Oh, I see what you mean.

CHARLOTTE: Max sees what I mean. All those people out front thinking, that's why she got the job. You're right, Max.

MAX: I never said anything!

CHARLOTTE: And also thinking that I'm *her* . . . coming in with my little suitcase and my duty-free bag—'It's me!'—ooh, it's her!—so that's what they're like at home—he's scintillating and she's scintillated. (HENRY *starts to speak.*) Look out, he's going to scintillate.

HENRY: How was it really?—last night.

CHARLOTTE: Not good. The stalls had a deserted look, about two-thirds, I should think. (*With false innocence.*) Oh, sorry, darling, is that what you meant?

MAX: (*Disapproving*) Honestly, Charlotte. It was all right, Henry, *really*. All the laughs were in place, for a Saturday night anyway, and I had someone who came round afterwards who said the reconciliation scene was extremely moving. Actually, that reminds me. They *did* say—I mean, it's a tiny thing but I thought I'd pass it on because I do feel rather the same way . . . I mean all that stuff about the Japanese and digital watches—they suddenly have no idea what I'm talking about, you see, and I thought if we could just try it one night without—

(HENRY *halts him, like a traffic policeman.*)

HENRY: Excuse me, Max.

(HENRY *turns to* CHARLOTTE.)

Two-thirds empty or two-thirds full?

(CHARLOTTE *laughs brazenly.*)

CHARLOTTE: Hard luck, Max. (*She toasts.*) Well, here's to closing night. To the collapse of *House of Cards*.

MAX: (*Shocked*) Charlotte!

CHARLOTTE: Well, you try playing the feed one night instead of acting Henry after a buck's fizz and two rewrites. All *his* laughs are in place all right. So's my groan. Groan, groan, they all go when they find out. Oh, *groan*, so she hasn't got a lover at all, eh? And they lose interest in me totally. I'm a

20

victim of Henry's fantasy—a quiet, faithful bird with an
interesting job, and a recipe drawer, and a stiff upper lip,
and two semi-stiff lower ones all trembling for him—'I'm
sorry if you've had a bad time . . . There's a right thing to
say now . . .'

MAX: Jesus, Charlotte—

CHARLOTTE: (*Quite genially*) Oh, shut up, Max. If he'd given her
a lover instead of a temporary passport, we'd be in a play.
But he could no more do that than he could architect a
hotel. Sorry, *an* hotel.

HENRY: It's a little early in the day for all this.

CHARLOTTE: No, darling, it's a little late.

HENRY: She's good, you know, she's awfully good. She gets it
from me.

CHARLOTTE: Oh, yes, without you I'd be like one of your women.
'Fancy a drink?' 'Let me get you a drink.' 'Care for a
drink?' That's Henry's idea of women's parts. Drinks and
feeds. That's the public parts. There's a feed, Henry.

HENRY: You know, this desert island thing has a lot to be said
for it.

CHARLOTTE: You'd go mad, darling.

HENRY: I was thinking of you, darling. You could have one of
my plays as your book.

CHARLOTTE: I'll have the one with the largest number of pages.

(MAX *interposes his body, as it were.*)

MAX: Er, where's young Deborah today?

CHARLOTTE: Who?

MAX: Debbie.

CHARLOTTE: (*Baffled*) Debbie?

MAX: Your daughter.

CHARLOTTE: Daughter? Daughter? Must be some mistake. No
place for children. Smart talk, that's the thing. Children are
so unsmart. Before you know where you are, the chat is all
about the price of sandals. Henry couldn't do that. He
doesn't like research.

HENRY: True.

CHARLOTTE: Can't have a lot of kids complicating the clean exit
with suitcase.

21

MAX: (*To* CHARLOTTE.) Lots of people don't have children, in real life. Me and Annie . . .

HENRY: Oh, don't—I told her once that lots of women were only good for fetching drinks, and she became quite unreasonable. (*Blithely, knowing what he is doing,* HENRY *holds his empty glass towards* CHARLOTTE.)
Is there any more of that?
MAX *glances at* CHARLOTTE *and hastily tries to defuse the bomb.*)

MAX: Let me . . .
(MAX *takes* HENRY's *glass and fills it from the bottle and the jug.*)

CHARLOTTE: Lots of *men* are only good for fetching drinks—why don't you write about *them*?
(MAX *hands the glass back to* HENRY.)

HENRY: (*Smiling up at* MAX) Terribly pleased you could come round.

CHARLOTTE: Oh, yes, you owe him a drink. I'm the victim of his fantasy, and you're quids in on it. What an ego trip! Having all the words to come back with just as you need them. That's the difference between plays and real life—thinking time, time to get your bottle back. 'Must say, I take my hat off to you, coming home with Rembrandt place mats for your mother.' You don't really think that if Henry caught me out with a lover, he'd sit around being witty about place mats? Like hell he would. He'd come apart like a pick-a-sticks. His sentence structure would go to pot, closely followed by his sphincter. You know that, don't you, Henry? Henry? No answer. Are you there, Henry? Say something witty.
(HENRY *turns his head to her.*)

HENRY: Is it anyone I know?

MAX: (*Starting to rise*) Well, look, thanks for the drink—

CHARLOTTE: Oh, sit down, Max, for God's sake, or he'll think it's you.
(MAX *subsides unhappily.*)

HENRY: Just kidding, Max. Badinage. You know, *dialogue*.
(*The doorbell rings.*)
See what I mean?

MAX: Annie said she'd come round if her committee finished early. She's on this Justice for Brodie Committee . . . you

22

know . . . (*Pause*) I'll go, should I?

HENRY: I'll go.

MAX: No, stay where you are, I'll see if it's her.

(MAX *goes out to the front door*.)

CHARLOTTE: Thanks very much. Anyone else coming?

HENRY: Just give them a Twiglet. They won't stay.

CHARLOTTE: What did you phone him for in the first place?

HENRY: Well, I only have to write it once. He has to show up every night. I had a conscience.

CHARLOTTE: Do you have a conscience about me too?

HENRY: Absolutely. You can have a Twiglet.

CHARLOTTE: Well, don't ask her about Brodie.

HENRY: Right.

CHARLOTTE: If she starts on about scapegoats and cover-ups, she'll get a Twiglet up her nostril.

HENRY: Right.

CHARLOTTE: (*Enthusiastically*) Darling! It's been ages!

(ANNIE *has entered, followed by* MAX. ANNIE *is carrying a carrier bag loaded with greengrocery*.)

ANNIE: Hello, Charlotte. This is jolly nice of you.

MAX: We can only stay a minute.

ANNIE: How are you, Henry?

HENRY: Fine.

MAX: Annie's stewarding at the protest meeting this afternoon, so we can't—

HENRY: Oh, do shut up. Don't take any notice of Max. I made him nervous.

ANNIE: What did you do to him?

HENRY: Nothing at all. I asked him if he was having an affair with Charlotte, and he was offended.

ANNIE: Was he?

HENRY: Apparently not. Been shopping?

ANNIE: Not exactly. I saw a place open on my way back and . . . Anyway, you might as well take it as an offering.

CHARLOTTE: (*Taking the bag from her and investigating it*) Darling, there was absolutely no need to bring . . . mushrooms?

ANNIE: Yes.

CHARLOTTE: (*Not quite behaving well*) And a turnip . . .

23

ANNIE: (*Getting unhappy*) And carrots . . . Oh, dear, it must look as if—

HENRY: Where's the meat?

CHARLOTTE: Shut up.

ANNIE: I wish I'd brought flowers now.

CHARLOTTE: This is much nicer.

HENRY: So original. I'll get a vase.

ANNIE: It's supposed to be crudités.

HENRY: Crudités! Perfect title for a pornographic revue.

CHARLOTTE: I'll make a dip.

MAX: We're not staying to eat, for heaven's sake.

HENRY: Just a quick dip.

ANNIE: Would you like *me* to?

CHARLOTTE: No, no. I know where everything is.

HENRY: Yes, Charlotte will provide dips for the crudity. She knows where everything is.

(CHARLOTTE *takes charge of the vegetables.* HENRY *gets a fourth glass.*)

Sit down, have some buck's fizz. I feel reckless, extravagant, famous, and I'm next week's castaway on *Desert Island Discs.* You can be my luxury if you like.

ANNIE: I'm not sure I'm one you can afford.

MAX: What are your eight records?

HENRY: This is the problem. I hate music.

CHARLOTTE: He likes pop music.

HENRY: You don't have to repeat everything I say.

MAX: I don't understand the problem.

CHARLOTTE: The problem is he's a snob without being an inverted snob. He's *ashamed* of liking pop music.

(CHARLOTTE *takes the vegetables out into the kitchen, closing the door.*)

HENRY: This is true. The trouble is I don't like the pop music which it's all right to like. You can have a bit of Pink Floyd shoved in between your symphonies and your Dame Janet Baker—that shows a refreshing breadth of taste or at least a refreshing candour—but *I* like Wayne Fontana and the Mindbenders doing 'Um Um Um Um Um Um'.

MAX: Doing what?

HENRY: That's the title. (*He demonstrates it.*) 'Um-Um-Um-Um-Um-Um'. I like Neil Sedaka. Do you remember 'Oh, Carol'?

MAX: For God's sake.

HENRY: (*Cheerfully*) Yes, I'm not very up to date. I like Herman's Hermits, and the Hollies, and the Everly Brothers, and Brenda Lee, and the Supremes . . . I don't mean everything they did. I don't like *artists*. I like singles.

MAX: This is sheer pretension.

HENRY: (*Insistently*) No. It *moves* me, the way people are supposed to be moved by *real* music. I was taken once to Covent Garden to hear a woman called Callas in a sort of foreign musical with no dancing which people were donating kidneys to get tickets for. The idea was that I would be cured of my strange disability. As though the place were a kind of Lourdes, except that instead of the front steps being littered with wooden legs, it would be tin ears. My illness at the time took the form of believing that the Righteous Brothers' recording of 'You've Lost that Lovin' Feelin' ' on the London label was possibly the most haunting, the most deeply moving noise ever produced by the human spirit, and this female vocalist person was going to set me right.

MAX: No good?

HENRY: Not even close. That woman would have had a job getting into the top thirty if she was *hyped*.

MAX: You preferred the Brothers.

HENRY: I did. Do you think there's something wrong with me?

MAX: Yes. I'd say you were a moron.

HENRY: What can I do?

MAX: There's nothing you can do.

HENRY: I mean about *Desert Island Discs*.

ANNIE: You know damned well what you should do.

HENRY: Cancel?

MAX: Actually, I remember it. (*He sings, badly.*) 'You've lost that lovin' feeling . . .'

HENRY: That's an idea—aversion therapy.

MAX: (*Sings*) '. . . that lovin' feeling . . . You've lost that lovin' feeling . . .'

HENRY: I think it's working.

MAX: (*Sings*) '. . . it's gorn, gorn, gorn . . . oh—oh—oh—yeah . . .'

HENRY: (*Happily*) God, it's *rubbish*! You've cracked it. Now do 'Oh Carol'.

MAX: I don't know that one.

HENRY: I'll play it for you.

MAX: I think I'll go and help Charlotte.

ANNIE: I should go.

MAX: No. I thought of it first.

(CHARLOTTE *enters, carrying a bowl.*)

CHARLOTTE: One dip.

MAX: I was coming to help.

CHARLOTTE: All right, you can chop.

MAX: Fine. Chop . . .

(MAX *goes out into the kitchen.* CHARLOTTE *places the bowl and is about to follow* MAX *out.* HENRY *dips his finger into the bowl and tastes the dip.*)

HENRY: It needs something.

CHARLOTTE: I beg your pardon?

HENRY: It needs something. A bit of interest. Garlic? Lemon juice? I don't know.

CHARLOTTE: (*Coldly*) Perhaps you should employ a cook.

HENRY: Surely that would be excessive—a cook who spends all her time emptying jars of mayonnaise and adding lemon juice? What would we do with the surplus?

CHARLOTTE: Presumably put it on stage with the rest of your stuff.

(CHARLOTTE *goes out into the kitchen, closing the door. Pause.*)

HENRY: Are you all right?

(ANNIE *nods.*)

ANNIE: Are you all right?

(HENRY *nods.*)

Touch me.

(HENRY *shakes his head.*)

Touch me.

HENRY: No.

ANNIE: Come on, touch me.

Help yourself.

Touch me anywhere you like.

26

HENRY: No.

ANNIE: Touch me.

HENRY: No.

ANNIE: Coward.

HENRY: I love you anyway.

ANNIE: Yes, say that.

HENRY: I love you.

ANNIE: Go on.

HENRY: I love you.

ANNIE: That's it.

HENRY: I love you.

ANNIE: Touch me then. They'll come in or they won't. Take a chance. Kiss me.

HENRY: For Christ's sake.

ANNIE: Quick one on the carpet then.

HENRY: You're crackers.

ANNIE: I'm not interested in your mind.

HENRY: Yes, you are.

ANNIE: No, I'm not, I lied to you.
  (*Pause.* HENRY *smiles at her.*)
  I hate Sunday.

HENRY: Thought I'd cheer you up with an obscene phone call, but Max got to it first, so I improvised.

ANNIE: I might have come round anyway. 'Hello, Henry, Charlotte, just passing, long time no see.'

HENRY: That would have been pushing it.

ANNIE: I'm in a mood to push it. Let's go while they're chopping turnips.

HENRY: You *are* crackers.

ANNIE: We'll go, and then it will be done. Max will suffer. Charlotte will make you suffer and get custody. You'll see Debbie on Sundays, and in three years she'll be at university not giving a damn either way.

HENRY: It's not just Debbie.

ANNIE: No, you want to give it time—

HENRY: Yes—

ANNIE: . . . time to go wrong, change, spoil. Then you'll know it wasn't the real thing.

27

HENRY: I don't steal other men's wives.

ANNIE: *Sod* you.

HENRY: You know what I mean.

ANNIE: Yes, you mean you love me but you don't want it to get around. Me and the Righteous Brothers. Well, sod you.

(*The kitchen door is flung open and* MAX *enters rather dramatically, bleeding from a cut finger.*)

MAX: Don't panic! Have you got a hankie?

ANNIE: Max?

(ANNIE *and* HENRY *respond appropriately, each searching for a handkerchief.* HENRY *produces one first, a clean white one, from his pocket.*)

HENRY: Here—

MAX: Thanks. No, let me—

ANNIE: Let me see.

MAX: It's all right, it's not as bad as it looks. (*To Henry.*) Typical of your bloody kitchen—all champagne and no elastoplast.

ANNIE: Poor love, just hold the cut for a while.

MAX: I think I'll put it back under the tap.

(*He moves towards the kitchen.*)

HENRY: Sorry about this, Max. She tried to do it to me once.

(MAX *leaves, leaving the door open.* HENRY *and* ANNIE'*s conversation is in no way furtive but pitched to acknowledge the open door.*)

ANNIE: I'm sorry.

HENRY: No, I'm sorry.

ANNIE: It's all right. Anything's all right.

(HENRY *moves forward and kisses her lightly.*)

HENRY: It'll get better.

ANNIE: How?

HENRY: Maybe we'll get found out.

ANNIE: Better to tell them. Whoever comes in first, eh? If it's Max, I'll tell him. If it's Charlotte, you start.

All right?

It's easy. Like Butch Cassidy and the Sundance Kid jumping off the cliff.

It's only a couple of marriages and a child.

All right?

28

(CHARLOTTE *enters from the kitchen, carrying a tray of chopped-up vegetables.*)

(*To* HENRY.) All right?

(*This is bold as brass and, consequently, safe as houses: in this way* ANNIE *and* HENRY *continue to speak quite privately to each other in the interstices of the general conversation, under or over the respective preoccupations of* CHARLOTTE *and* MAX.)

CHARLOTTE: Did Max tell you? It's red cabbage. I've taken him off the knives. He's making another dip. He says it's Hawaiian. It's supposed to be served in an empty pineapple. We haven't got a pineapple. He's going to serve it in an empty tin of pineapple chunks. I do envy you being married to a man with a sense of humour. Henry thinks he has a sense of humour, but what he has is a joke reflex. Eh, Henry? His mind is racing. Pineapple, pineapple . . . Come on, darling.

HENRY: (*To* ANNIE.) No. Sorry.

ANNIE: It's all right.

CHARLOTTE: (*Busy with cutlery*) Is Debbie expecting lunch?

HENRY: (*To* ANNIE.) No.

CHARLOTTE: What?

HENRY: No. She wants to stay out.

(ANNIE *drinks what remains in her glass.*)

ANNIE: Where is Debbie?

HENRY: Riding school. Drink?

(HENRY *takes her empty glass out of her hand.*)

ANNIE: Love you.

CHARLOTTE: She used to eat like a horse, till she had one.

(HENRY *refills* ANNIE'S *glass.*)

HENRY: I'm picking her up this afternoon.

(*He returns* ANNIE'S *glass.*)

Buck's fizz all right?

CHARLOTTE: Picking her up?

ANNIE: I don't care.

(MAX *enters with the Hawaiian dip in the pineapple tin.*)

MAX: Here we are.

ANNIE: Anything's all right.

MAX: It's Hawaiian.

HENRY: You're a lovely feller.

CHARLOTTE: Well done, Max.

ANNIE: So are you.

(*She meets* MAX, *dips her finger into the tin and tastes the dip.*)

MAX: I hope I've got it right. What do you think?

(*In his other hand* MAX *has* HENRY's *somewhat blood-stained handkerchief, which he now offers back.*)

(*To Henry.*) Thanks. What should I do with it?

HENRY: (*Taking it*) It's okay, I'll take it.

(HENRY *puts the handkerchief in his pocket.*)

ANNIE: (*To* MAX.) Not bad. (*To* CHARLOTTE.) May I?

CHARLOTTE: Feel free.

ANNIE: Hang on a sec.

(*She takes the tin from* MAX *and leaves the room with it, going to the kitchen.*)

CHARLOTTE: (*To* HENRY.) You're over-protective. She could walk it in half an hour.

MAX: Who, what?

CHARLOTTE: Debbie.

HENRY: By the time she finished mucking out, whatever they call it . . .

CHARLOTTE: Grooming the mount, mounting the groom . . .

HENRY: (*Unamused*) Hilarious.

MAX: *I* wouldn't let her walk. Someone got murdered on the common not long ago. Mustn't put temptation in the way.

CHARLOTTE: Debbie wouldn't murder anyone. She'd just duff them up a little bit. I can't make her out at all.

(ANNIE *re-enters with the dip.*)

Some people have daughters who love ponies.

(*Passing* HENRY, ANNIE *casually puts her finger in his mouth, without pausing.*)

ANNIE: What do you think?

CHARLOTTE: Some people have daughters who go punk. We've got one who goes riding on Barnes Common looking like the Last of the Mohicans.

HENRY: Crackers.

(ANNIE *delivers the dip to* CHARLOTTE.)

CHARLOTTE: (*To* ANNIE.) Is yours a case of sperm count or

twisted tubes? Or is it that you just can't stand the little buggers?

MAX: Charlotte!

HENRY: What business is that of yours?

CHARLOTTE: He's in love with his, you know.

ANNIE: Isn't that supposed to be normal?

CHARLOTTE: No, dear, normal is the other way round.

HENRY: I say, Annie, what's this Brodie Committee all about? Charlotte was asking.

MAX: You know, Private Brodie.

ANNIE: It's all right.

MAX: Annie knows him.

ANNIE: I don't know him.

MAX: Tell them about meeting him on the train.

ANNIE: Yes. I met him on a train.

(*Pause. But* HENRY, *exhibiting avid interest, disobliges her.*)

HENRY: Yes?

ANNIE: (*Laughs uncomfortably*) I seem to have told this story before.

HENRY: But we haven't seen you for ages.

MAX: Annie was travelling up to London from our cottage, weren't you?

HENRY: *Were* you?

ANNIE: Yes.

HENRY: (*Fascinated*) You have a cottage in . . .?

ANNIE: Norfolk.

HENRY: Norfolk! What, up in the hills there?

ANNIE: (*Testily*) *What* hills? Norfolk is absolutely—
(*She brings herself up short.*)

CHARLOTTE: Oh, very funny. Stop it, Henry.

HENRY: I have no idea what you are talking about. So, you were coming up to London from your flat in Norfolk—*cottage*— and you met this Private Brodie on the train.

ANNIE: Yes.

MAX: It was quite remarkable. Brodie was on his way to the anti-missiles demonstration, just like Annie.

HENRY: *Really?*

ANNIE: Yes.

31

HENRY: How did you know?

Was he wearing a 'Missiles Out' badge on his uniform?

ANNIE: He wasn't in uniform.

MAX: The guts of it, the sheer moral courage. An ordinary soldier using his weekend pass to demonstrate against their bloody missiles.

HENRY: *Their?* I thought they were ours.

MAX: No, they're American.

HENRY: Oh, yes—*their* . . .

MAX: Pure moral conscience, you see—I mean, he didn't have our motivation.

HENRY: *Our?*

MAX: Mine and Annie's.

(HENRY *appears not to understand.*)

Owning property in Little Barmouth.

HENRY: Yes, of course. Private Brodie didn't own a weekend cottage in Little Barmouth, you mean.

MAX: No, he's a Scots lad. He was stationed at the camp down the road. He was practically guarding the base where these rockets are making Little Barmouth into a sitting duck for the Russian counter-attack, should it ever come to that.

HENRY: (*To* ANNIE.) I see what you mean.

ANNIE: Do you?

HENRY: Well, yes. Little Barmouth isn't going to declare war on Russia, so why should Little Barmouth be wiped out in a war not of Little Barmouth's making?

MAX: Quite.

CHARLOTTE: Shut up, Henry.

MAX: Is he being like that?

CHARLOTTE: Yes, he's being like that.

MAX: I don't see what he's got to be like that about.

HENRY: (*Capitulating enthusiastically*) Absolutely! So you met this Private Brodie on the train, and Brodie said, 'I see you're going to the demo down Whitehall.' Right?

ANNIE: No. He recognized me from my children's serial. He used to watch *Rosie of the Royal Infirmary* when he was a kid.

MAX: How *about* that? It seems like the day before yesterday Annie was doing *Rosie of the Royal Infirmary*. He's *still* a kid.

ANNIE: Yes. Twenty-one.

MAX: He's a child.

HENRY: He kicked two policemen inside out, didn't he?

MAX: Piss off.

(*To* CHARLOTTE.) If you want to know what it's all about, you should come to the meeting.

CHARLOTTE: I know I should, but I like to keep my Sundays free. For entertaining friends, I mean. Fortunately, there are people like Annie to make up for people like me.

HENRY: Perhaps I'll go.

CHARLOTTE: No, you're people like me. You tell him, Annie.

ANNIE: You're picking up Debbie from riding school.

CHARLOTTE: When Henry comes across a phrase like 'the caring society' he scrunches up the *Guardian* and draws his knees up into his chest.

HENRY: That's merely professional fastidiousness. Yes, come to that, I think I'll join the Justice for Brodie Committee. I should have thought of that before.

CHARLOTTE: They don't want dilettantes. You have to be properly motivated, like Annie.

HENRY: I don't see that my motivation matters a damn. Least of all to Brodie. He just wants to get out of jail. What does he care if we're motivated by the wrong reasons.

MAX: Like what?

HENRY: Like the desire to be taken for properly motivated members of the caring society. One of us is probably kicking his father, a policeman. Another is worried that his image is getting a bit too right-of-centre. Another is in love with a committee member and wishes to gain her approbation . . .

CHARLOTTE: Which one are you?

HENRY: You think I'm kidding, but I'm not. Public postures have the configuration of private derangement.

MAX: Who said that?

HENRY: I did, you fool.

MAX: I mean first.

HENRY: Oh, first. (*To* ANNIE.) Take him off to your meeting, I'm sick of him.

ANNIE: He's not coming.

33

HENRY: (*Savouring it*) You are not going to the meeting?

MAX: No, actually. Not that I wouldn't, but it would mean letting down my squash partner.

HENRY: Squash partner? An interesting moral dilemma. I wonder what Saint Augustine would have done?

MAX: I don't think Saint Augustine had a squash partner.

HENRY: I know that. Nobody would play with him. Even so. I put myself in his place. I balance a pineapple chunk on my carrot. I ponder. On the one hand, Max's squash partner. Decent chap but not a deprivation of the first magnitude. And on the other hand, Brodie, an out-and-out thug, an arsonist, vandalizer of a national shrine, *but* mouldering in jail for years to come owing, *perhaps,* to society's inability to comprehend a man divided against himself, a pacifist hooligan.

MAX: I don't condone vandalism, however idealistic. I just—

HENRY: Yes, well, as acts of vandalism go, starting a fire on the Cenotaph using the wreath to the Unknown Soldier as kindling scores very low on discretion. I assumed he was trying to be provocative.

MAX: Of course he was, you idiot. But he got hammered by an emotional backlash.

HENRY: No, no, you *can't*—

MAX: Yes, he bloody was!

HENRY: I mean 'hammer' and 'backlash'. You can't *do it*!

MAX: Oh, for Christ's sake. This is your house, and I'm drinking your wine, but if you don't mind me saying so, Henry—

HENRY: *My* saying, Max.

MAX: Right.

(*He puts down his glass definitively and stands up.*)

Come on, Annie.

There's something wrong with you.

You've got something missing. You may have all the answers, but having all the answers is not what life's about.

HENRY: I'm sorry, but it actually *hurts*.

MAX: Brodie may be no intellectual, like you, but he did march for a cause, and now he's got six years for a stupid piece of bravado and a punch-up, and he'd have been forgotten

in a week if it wasn't for Annie. That's what life's about—
messy bits of good and bad luck, and people caring and not
necessarily having all the answers. Who the hell are you to
patronize Annie? She's worth ten of you.

HENRY: I know that.

MAX: I'm sorry, Charlotte.

CHARLOTTE: Well done, Henry.

(MAX *leaves towards the front door.* CHARLOTTE, *with a glance
at* HENRY, *rolling her eyes in rebuke, follows him out of the
room.* ANNIE *stands up. For the rest of the scene she is moving,
hardly looking at* HENRY, *perhaps fetching her handbag.*)

HENRY: It was just so I could look at you without it looking funny.

ANNIE: What time are you going for Debbie?

HENRY: Four o'clock. Why?

ANNIE: Three o'clock. Look for my car.

HENRY: What about Brodie?

ANNIE: Let him rot.

(ANNIE *leaves, closing the door. Pop music: Herman's Hermits,
'I'm Into Something Good'.*)

SCENE THREE

MAX *and* ANNIE.

A living-room.

MAX *is alone, listening to a small radio, from which Herman's Hermits
continue to be heard, at an adjusted level. The disposition of furniture
and doors makes the scene immediately reminiscent of the beginning of
Scene 1. The front door, off stage, is heard being opened with a key.
The door closes.* ANNIE, *wearing a topcoat, appears briefly round the
door to the hall. She is in a hurry.*

ANNIE: Have you got it on?

(*She disappears and reappears without the coat.*)

How much have I missed?

MAX: Five or ten minutes.

ANNIE: Damn. If I'd had the car, I'd have caught the beginning.

35

MAX: Where have you been?

ANNIE: You know where I've been. Rehearsing.

(*The music ends and is followed by* HENRY *being interviewed on* Desert Island Discs, *but the radio dialogue, during the few moments before* MAX *turns the sound down, is meaningless under the stage dialogue.*)

MAX: How's Julie?

ANNIE: Who?

MAX: Julie. Miss Julie. Strindberg's Miss Julie. Miss Julie by August Strindberg, how is she?

ANNIE: Are you all right?

MAX: This probably—

ANNIE: Shush up.

MAX: This probably isn't anything, but—

ANNIE: *Max, can I listen?*

(MAX *turns the radio sound right down.*)

What's up? Are you cross?

MAX: This probably isn't anything, but I found this in the car, between the front seats.

(*He shows her a soiled and blood-stained white handkerchief.*)

ANNIE: What is it?

MAX: Henry's handkerchief.

ANNIE: Well, give it back to him.

(*She reaches for it.*)

Here, I'll wash it and you can give it to Charlotte at the theatre.

MAX: I did give it back to him.

When was he in the car?

(*Pause*)

It was a clean handkerchief, apart from my blood.

Have you got a cold?

It looks filthy. It's dried filthy.

You're filthy.

You filthy cow.

You rotten filthy—

(*He starts to cry, barely audible, immobile.* ANNIE *waits. He recovers his voice.*)

It's not true, is it?

ANNIE: Yes.

MAX: Oh, God.

(*He stands up.*)

Why did you?

ANNIE: I'm awfully sorry, Max—

MAX: (*Interrupting, suddenly pulled together*) All right. It happened. All right. It didn't mean anything.

ANNIE: I'm awfully sorry, Max, but I love him.

MAX: Oh, no.

ANNIE: Yes.

MAX: Oh, *no*. You don't.

ANNIE: Yes, I do. And he loves me. That's that, isn't it? I'm sorry it's awful. But it's better really. All that lying.

MAX: (*Breaking up again*) Oh, Christ, Annie, stop it. I love you. Please don't—

ANNIE: Come on, please—it doesn't have to be like this.

MAX: How long for? And *him*—oh, *God*.

(*He kicks the radio savagely. The radio has gone into music again—the Righteous Brothers singing 'You've Lost That Lovin' Feelin' '—and* MAX's *kick has the effect of turning up the volume rather loud. He flings himself upon* ANNIE *in something like an assault which turns immediately into an embrace.* ANNIE *does no more than suffer the embrace, looking over* MAX's *shoulder, her face blank.*)

SCENE FOUR

HENRY *and* ANNIE.

Living-room. Obviously temporary and makeshift quarters, divided Left and Right by a clothes rail, making two areas, 'his' and 'hers'. HENRY *is alone, writing at a desk.*

The disposition of door and furniture makes the scene immediately reminiscent of Scene 2. On the floor are a number of cardboard boxes containing files, papers, letters, scripts, bills . . . The pillage of a filing system. There is also a couch. The Sunday newspapers and a bound script are on or near the couch.

37

A radio plays pop music quietly while HENRY *writes.*
ANNIE *enters from the bedroom door, barefoot and wearing* HENRY's *robe, which is too big for her.* HENRY, *in mid-sentence, looks up briefly and looks down again.*

ANNIE: I'm not here. Promise.
> (*She goes to the couch and carefully opens a newspaper.* HENRY *continues to write.* ANNIE *glances towards him once or twice. He takes no notice. She stands up and goes behind his chair, looking over his shoulder as he works. He takes no notice. She goes round the desk and stands in front of him. He takes no notice. She flashes open the robe for his benefit. He takes no notice. She moves round behind him again and looks over his shoulder. He turns and grabs her with great suddenness, causing her to scream and laugh. The assault turns into a standing embrace.*)

HENRY: You're a bloody nuisance.
ANNIE: Sorry, sorry, sorry. I'll be good. I'll sit and learn my script.
HENRY: No, you won't.
ANNIE: I'll go in the other room.
HENRY: This room will do.
ANNIE: No, you've got to do my play.
HENRY: I can't write it. Let me off.
ANNIE: No, you promised. It's my gift.
HENRY: All right. Stay and talk a minute. (*He turns off the radio.*) Raw material, then I'll do this page, then I'll rape you, then I'll do the page again, then I'll—Oh (*happily*), are you all right?
> (ANNIE *nods.*)

ANNIE: Yeah. Are you all right?
> (*He nods.*)
> (*Gleefully, self-reproachful.*) Isn't it awful? Max is so unhappy while I feel so . . . *thrilled.* His misery just seems . . . not in very good taste. Am I awful? He leaves letters for me at rehearsal, you know, and gets me to come to the phone by pretending to be my agent and people. He loves me, and he wants to punish me with his pain, but I can't come up with the proper guilt. I'm sort of irritated by it. It's so *tiring* and

38

so *uninteresting*. You never write about that, you lot.

HENRY: What?

ANNIE: Gallons of ink and miles of typewriter ribbon expended on the misery of the unrequited lover; not a word about the utter tedium of the unrequiting. It's a very interesting . . .

HENRY: Lacuna?

ANNIE: What? No, I mean it's a very interesting sort of . . .

HENRY: Prejudice?

ANNIE: It's a very interesting . . . thing.

HENRY: Yes, thing.

ANNIE: No, I mean it shows—never mind—I've lost it now.

HENRY: How are you this morning?

ANNIE: One behind. Where were you?

HENRY: You were flat out.

ANNIE: Your own fault. When I take a Mog, I'm on the downhill slope. You should have come to bed when you said.

HENRY: (*Indicating his desk*) It wasn't where I could leave it. I would have gone to sleep depressed.

ANNIE: Well, I thought, the honeymoon is over. Fifteen days and fuckless to bye-byes.

HENRY: No, actually, I managed.

ANNIE: You did not.

HENRY: Yes, I did. You were totally zonked. Only your reflexes were working.

ANNIE: Liar.

HENRY: Honestly.

ANNIE: Why didn't you wake me?

HENRY: I thought I'd try it without you talking.

Look, I'm not doing any good, why don't we—?

ANNIE: You rotter. Just for that I'm going to learn my script.

HENRY: I'll read in for you.

(*She glowers at him but finds a page in the script and hands the script to him.*)

ANNIE: You didn't really, did you?

HENRY: Yes.

(*She 'reads' without inflection.*)

ANNIE: '*Très gentil, Monsieur Jean, très gentil!*'

39

HENRY: (*Reading*) '*Vous voulez plaisanter, madame!*'

ANNIE: '*Et vous voulez parler français?* Where did you pick that up?'

HENRY: 'In Switzerland. I worked as a waiter in one of the best hotels in Lucerne.'

ANNIE: 'You're quite the gentleman in that coat . . . *charmant*.' You rotter.

HENRY: 'You flatter me, Miss Julie.'

ANNIE: 'Flatter? I flatter?'

HENRY: 'I'd like to accept the compliment, but modesty forbids. And, of course, my modesty entails your insincerity. Hence, you flatter me.'

ANNIE: 'Where did you learn to talk like that? Do you spend a lot of time at the theatre?'

HENRY: 'Oh yes. I get about, you know.'

ANNIE: Oh, Hen. Are you all right?

HENRY: Not really. I can't do mine. I don't know how to write love. I try to write it properly, and it just comes out embarrassing. It's either childish or it's rude. And the rude bits are absolutely juvenile. I can't use any of it. My credibility is already hanging by a thread after *Desert Island Discs*. Anyway, I'm too prudish. Perhaps I should write it completely artificial. Blank verse. Poetic imagery. Not so much of the 'Will you still love me when my tits are droopy?' 'Of course I will, darling, it's your bum I'm mad for', and more of the 'By my troth, thy beauty makest the moon hide her radiance', do you think?

ANNIE: Not really, no.

HENRY: No. Not really. I don't know. Loving and being loved is unliterary. It's happiness expressed in banality and lust. It makes me nervous to see three-quarters of a page and no *writing* on it. I mean, I *talk* better than this.

ANNIE: You'll have to learn to do sub-text. My Strindberg is steaming with lust, but there is nothing rude on the page. We just talk round it. Then he sort of bites my finger and I do the heavy breathing and he gives me a quick feel, kisses me on the neck . . .

HENRY: Who does?

ANNIE: Gerald. It's all very exciting.
(HENRY *laughs, immoderately, and* ANNIE *continues coldly*.)
Or amusing, of course.
HENRY: We'll do that bit . . . you breathe, I'll feel . . . (*She pushes him away*.)
ANNIE: Go away. You'll just get moody afterwards.
HENRY: When was I ever moody?
ANNIE: Whenever you get seduced from your work.
HENRY: You mean the other afternoon?
ANNIE: What other afternoon? No, I don't mean *seduced*, for God's sake. Can't you think about anything else?
HENRY: Certainly. Like what?
ANNIE: I mean 'seduced', like when you're seduced by someone on the television.
HENRY: I've never been seduced on the television.
ANNIE: You were seduced by Miranda Jessop on the television.
HENRY: Professional duty.
ANNIE: If she hadn't been in it, you wouldn't have watched that play if they'd come round and done it for you on your carpet.
HENRY: Exactly. I had a postcard from her agent, would I be sure to watch her this week in *Trotsky Playhouse* or whatever they call it.
ANNIE: You only looked up when she stripped off. Think I can't see through you? That's why I took my Mog. Sod you, I thought, feel free.
HENRY: You're daft. I've got to watch her if she's going to do my telly. It's just good manners.
ANNIE: *Her* tits are droopy already.
HENRY: I'm supposed to have an opinion, you see.
ANNIE: I think she's bloody overrated, as a matter of fact.
HENRY: I have to agree. I wouldn't give them more than six out of ten.
(*She clouts him with her script*.)
Four.
(*She clouts him again*.)
Three.
ANNIE: You think you're so bloody funny.

41

HENRY: What's up with you? I hardly know the woman.

ANNIE: You'll like her. She wears leopard-skin pants.

HENRY: How do you know?

ANNIE: I shared a dressing-room with her.

HENRY: I don't suppose she wears them all the time.

ANNIE: I'm bloody sure she doesn't.

HENRY: 'By my troth thy beauty makest the moon—'

ANNIE: Oh, shut up.

HENRY: What are you jealous about?

ANNIE: I'm not jealous.

HENRY: All right, what are you cross about?

ANNIE: I'm not cross. Do your work.

(*She makes a show of concentrating on her script.* HENRY *makes a show of resuming work. Pause.*)

HENRY: I'm sorry.

ANNIE: What for?

HENRY: I don't know.

I'll have to be going out to pick up Debbie. I don't want to go if we're not friends.

Will you come, then?

ANNIE: No. It was a mistake last time. It spoils it for her, being nervous.

HENRY: She wasn't nervous.

ANNIE: Not her. You.

(*Pause*)

HENRY: Well, I'll be back around two.

ANNIE: I won't be here.

(*Pause*)

HENRY: (*Remembering*) Oh, yes. Is it today you're going prison-visiting? You're being very—um—faithful to Brodie.

ANNIE: That surprises you, does it?

HENRY: I only mean that you haven't got much time for good causes. You haven't got a weekend cottage either.

ANNIE: You think I'm more like you.

HENRY: Yes.

ANNIE: It's just that I happen to know him.

HENRY: You don't know him. You met him on a train.

ANNIE: Well, he's the only political prisoner I've ever met on a train. He's lucky.

HENRY: Political?

ANNIE: It was a political act which got him jumped on by the police in the first place so it's . . .

HENRY: A priori?

ANNIE: No, it's—

HENRY: De facto?

ANNIE: It's common sense that resisting arrest isn't the same as a criminal doing it.

HENRY: Arson is a criminal offence.

ANNIE: Arson is burning down buildings. Setting fire to the wreath on the Cenotaph is a symbolic act. Surely you can see the difference?

HENRY: (*Carefully*) Oh, yes . . . That's . . . easy to see.

(*Not carefully enough.* ANNIE *looks at him narrowly.*)

ANNIE: And, of course, he did get hammered by an emotional backlash.

(*Pause*)

HENRY: Do you mean real leopard skin or just printed nylon?

(*She erupts and assails him, shouting.*)

ANNIE: You don't love me the way I love you. I'm just a relief after Charlotte, and a novelty.

HENRY: You're a novelty all right. I never *met* anyone so silly. I love you. I don't know why you're behaving like this.

ANNIE: I'm behaving normally. It's you who's abnormal. You don't care enough to *care*. Jealousy is normal.

HENRY: I thought you said you *weren't* jealous.

ANNIE: Well, why aren't *you* ever jealous?

HENRY: Of whom?

ANNIE: Of anybody. You don't care if Gerald Jones sticks his tongue in my ear—which, incidentally, he does whenever he gets the chance.

HENRY: Is that what this is all about?

ANNIE: It's insulting the way you just laugh.

HENRY: But you've got no interest in him.

ANNIE: I know that, but why should you assume it?

HENRY: Because you haven't. This is stupid.

ANNIE: But why don't you *mind*?

43

HENRY: I do.

ANNIE: No, you don't.

HENRY: That's true, I don't.

Why *is* that?

It's because I feel superior. There he is, poor bugger, picking up the odd crumb of ear wax from the rich man's table. You're right. I don't mind. I like it. I like the way his presumption admits his poverty. I like him, knowing that that's all there is, because you're coming home to me and we don't want anyone else.

I love love. I love having a lover and being one. The insularity of passion. I love it. I love the way it blurs the distinction between everyone who isn't one's lover.

Only two kinds of presence in the world. There's you and there's them.

I love you so.

ANNIE: I love you so, Hen.

(*They kiss. The alarm on* HENRY'*s wristwatch goes off. They separate.*)

HENRY: Sorry.

ANNIE: Don't get kicked by the horse.

HENRY: Don't get kicked by Brodie.

(*He goes to the door to leave. At the door he looks at her and nods. She nods at him. He leaves.*

ANNIE *goes slowly to* HENRY'*s desk and looks at the pages on it. She turns on the radio and turns it from pop to Bach. She goes back to the desk and, almost absently, opens one of the drawers. Leaving it open, she goes to the door and disappears briefly into the hall, then reappears, closing the door. She goes to one of the cardboard boxes on the floor. She removes the contents from the box. She places the pile of papers on the floor. Squatting down, she starts going through the pile, methodically and unhurriedly. The radio plays on.*)

ACT TWO

SCENE FIVE

HENRY *and* ANNIE.
Living-room/study. Three doors.
Two years later. A different house. The two years ought to show on
HENRY *and on* ANNIE. *Perhaps he now uses glasses when he is reading,*
as he is at the beginning of the scene, or he may even have grown a
moustache. ANNIE *may have cut her hair short. Opera (Verdi) is*
playing on the record player. There is a TV and video and a small
radio on HENRY's *desk, on which there is also a typewriter.* HENRY
is alone, reading a script which consists of a sheaf of typed pages.
HENRY *reads for a few moments.*
ANNIE *enters from bedroom or kitchen and glances at* HENRY, *not*
casually, then sits down and watches him read for a moment. Then
she looks away and listens to the music for a moment. HENRY *glances*
up at her.
ANNIE *looks at him.*

ANNIE: Well?
HENRY: Oh—um—Strauss.
ANNIE: What?
HENRY: Not Strauss.
ANNIE: I meant the play.
HENRY: (*Indicating the script*) Ah. The play.
ANNIE: (*Scornfully*) Strauss. How can it be Strauss? It's in
Italian.
HENRY: Is it? (*He listens.*) So it is.
Italian opera.
One of the Italian operas.
Verdi.

45

ANNIE: Which one?

HENRY: Giuseppe.

(*He judges from her expression that this is not the right answer.*)

Monty?

ANNIE: I mean which *opera*.

HENRY: Ah. (*Confidently*) *Madame Butterfly*.

ANNIE: You're doing it on purpose.

(*She goes to the record player and stops it playing.*)

HENRY: I promise you.

ANNIE: You'd think that *something* would have sunk in after two years and a bit.

HENRY: I like it—I really do like it—quite, it's just that I can't tell them apart. Two years and a bit isn't very long when they're all going for the same sound. Actually, I've got a better ear than you—*you* can't tell the difference between the Everly Brothers and the Andrews Sisters.

ANNIE: There isn't any difference.

HENRY: Or we could split up. Can we have something decent on now?

ANNIE: No.

HENRY: All right. Put on one of your instrumental numbers. The big band sound. (*He does the opening of Beethoven's Fifth.*) Da—da—da—*dah* . . .

ANNIE: Get *on*.

HENRY: Right.

(*He turns his attention to the script.*)

Stop me if anybody has said this before, but it's interesting how many of the all time greats begin with B: Beethoven. the Big Bopper . . .

ANNIE: That's all they have in common.

HENRY: I wouldn't say that. They're both dead. The Big Bopper died in the same plane crash that killed Buddy Holly and Richie Valens, you know.

ANNIE: No, I didn't know. Have you given up on the play or what?

HENRY: Buddy Holly was twenty-two. Think of what he might have gone on to achieve. I mean, if Beethoven had been

46

killed in a plane crash at twenty-two, the history of music would have been very different. As would the history of aviation, of course.

ANNIE: *Henry*.

HENRY: The play.

(*He turns his attention back to the script.*)

ANNIE: How far have you got?

HENRY: Do you have a professional interest in this or is it merely personal?

ANNIE: Merely?

(*Pause*)

HENRY: Do you have a personal interest in this or is it merely professional?

ANNIE: Which one are you dubious about?

(*Pause*)

HENRY: Pause.

ANNIE: I could do her, couldn't I?

HENRY: Mary? Oh, sure—without make-up.

ANNIE: Well, then. *Three Sisters* is definitely up the spout.

HENRY: Nothing's definite with that lot.

ANNIE: The other two are pregnant.

HENRY: Half a dozen new lines could take care of that.

ANNIE: If this script could be in a fit state, say, a month from now—

HENRY: Anyway, I thought you were committing incest in Glasgow.

ANNIE: I haven't said I'll do it.

HENRY: I think you should. It's classy stuff, Webster. I love all that Jacobean sex and violence.

ANNIE: It's Ford, not Webster. It's Elizabethan, not Jacobean. *And* it's Glasgow.

HENRY: Don't you work north of Cambridge Circus, then?

ANNIE: I was thinking you might miss me—pardon my mistake.

HENRY: I was thinking you might like me to come with you— pardon mine.

ANNIE: You hadn't the faintest intention of coming to Glasgow for five weeks.

HENRY: That's true. I answered out of panic. Of course I'd miss you.

ANNIE: Also, it *is* somewhat north.

(HENRY *'shoots' her between the eyes with his forefinger.*)

HENRY: Got you. Is it rehearsing in Glasgow?

ANNIE: (*Nods*) After the first week. (*Indicating the script.*) Where've you got to?

HENRY: They're on the train.

'You're a strange boy, Billy. How old are you?'

'Twenty. But I've lived more than you'll ever live.'

Should I read out loud?

ANNIE: If you like.

HENRY: Give you the feel of it.

ANNIE: All right.

HENRY: I'll go back a bit . . . where they first meet. All right?

(ANNIE *nods.* HENRY *makes train noises. She is defensive, not quite certain whether he is being wicked or not.*)

(*Reading*) 'Excuse me, is this seat taken?'

'No.'

'Mind if I sit down?'

'It's a free country.'

'Thank you.'

'(*He sits down opposite her. Mary carries on with reading her book.*)'

'Going far?'

'To London.'

'So, you were saying . . . So you think it's a free country.'

'Don't you?'

'This is it, we're all free to do as we're told. My name's Bill, by the way. What's yours?'

'Mary.'

'I'm glad to make your acquaintance, Mary.'

'I'm glad to make yours, Bill.'

'Do you know what time this train is due to arrive in London?'

'At about half-past one, I believe, if it is on time.'

'You put me in mind of Mussolini, Mary. Yes, you look just like him, you've got the same eyes.'

48

ANNIE: If you're not going to read it properly, don't bother.

HENRY: Sorry.

'At about half-past one, I believe, if it is on time.'

'You put me in mind of Mussolini, Mary. People used to say about Mussolini, he may be a Fascist, but at least the trains run on time. Makes you wonder why British Rail isn't totally on time, eh?'

'What do you mean?'

'I mean it's a funny thing. The Fascists are in charge but the trains are late often as not.'

'But this isn't a Fascist country.'

'Are you quite sure of that, Mary? Take the army—'

You're not going to do this, are you?

ANNIE: Why not?

HENRY: It's no good.

ANNIE: You mean it's not literary.

HENRY: It's not literary, and it's no good. He can't write.

ANNIE: You're a snob.

HENRY: I'm a snob, and he can't write.

ANNIE: I know it's raw, but he's got something to say.

HENRY: He's got something to say. It happens to be something extremely silly and bigoted. But leaving that aside, there is still the problem that he can't write. He can burn things down, but he can't write.

ANNIE: Give it back. I shouldn't have asked you.

HENRY: For God's sake, Annie, if it wasn't Brodie you'd never have got through it.

ANNIE: But it *is* Brodie. That's the point. Two and a half years ago he could hardly put six words together.

HENRY: He still can't.

ANNIE: You *pig*.

HENRY: I'm a pig, and he can't—

ANNIE: I'll smash you one. It's you who's bigoted. You're bigoted about what writing is supposed to be like. You judge everything as though everyone starts off from the same place, aiming at the same prize. Eng. Lit. Shakespeare out in front by a mile, and the rest of the field strung out behind trying to close the gap. You all write for people who would

49

like to write like you if only they could write. Well, sod you, and sod Eng. sodding Lit.!

HENRY: Right.

ANNIE: Brodie isn't writing to compete like you. He's writing to be heard.

HENRY: Right.

ANNIE: And he's done it on his own.

HENRY: Yes. Yes . . . I can see he's done a lot of reading.

ANNIE: You can't expect it to be Eng. Lit.

HENRY: No.

ANNIE: He's a prisoner shouting over the wall.

HENRY: Quite. Yes, I see what you mean.

ANNIE: Oh shut up! I can't bear you agreeing with me just to keep me quiet. I'd rather have your sarcasm.

HENRY: Why a play? Did you suggest it?

ANNIE: Not exactly.

HENRY: Why did you?

ANNIE: The committee, what's left of it, thought . . . I mean, people have got bored with Brodie. People get bored with anything after two or three years. The campaign needs . . .

HENRY: A shot in the arm?

ANNIE: No, it needs . . .

HENRY: A kick up the arse?

ANNIE: (*Flares*) For Christ's sake, will you stop finishing my sentences for me!

HENRY: Sorry.

ANNIE: I've lost it now.

HENRY: The campaign needs . . .

ANNIE: A writer is harder to ignore. I thought, TV plays get talked about, make some impact. Get his case reopened. Do you think? I mean, Henry, what *do* you think?

HENRY: I think it makes a lot of sense.

ANNIE: No, what do you *really* think?

HENRY: Oh, *really* think. Well, I *really* think writing rotten plays is not in itself proof of rehabilitation. Still less of wrongful conviction. But even if it were, I think that anyone who thinks that they're bored with Brodie won't know what boredom is till they've sat through his apologia. Not that

50

anyone will get the chance, because it's half as long as *Das Kapital* and only twice as funny. I also think you should know better.

ANNIE: You arrogant sod.

HENRY: You swear too much.

ANNIE: Roger is willing to do it, in principle.

HENRY: What Roger? Oh *Roger*. Why the hell would Roger do it?

ANNIE: He's on the committee.

(HENRY *looks at the ceiling.*)

It just needs a bit of work.

HENRY: You're all bent.

ANNIE: You're jealous.

HENRY: Of Brodie?

ANNIE: You're jealous of the idea of the writer. You want to keep it sacred, special, not something anybody can do. Some of us have it, some of us don't. *We* write, *you* get written about. What gets you about Brodie is he doesn't know his place. You say he can't write like a head waiter saying you can't come in here without a tie. Because he can't put words together. What's so good about putting words together?

HENRY: It's traditionally considered advantageous for a writer.

ANNIE: He's not a writer. He's a convict. *You're* a writer. You write *because* you're a writer. Even when you write *about* something, you have to think up something to write about just so you can keep writing. More well chosen words nicely put together. So what? Why should that be *it*? Who says?

HENRY: Nobody says. It just works best.

ANNIE: Of *course* it works. You teach a lot of people what to expect from good writing, and you end up with a lot of people saying you write well. Then somebody who isn't in on the game comes along, like Brodie, who really has something to write about, something real, and you can't get through it. Well, *he* couldn't get through *yours*, so where are you? To you, he can't write. To him, write is all you *can* do.

HENRY: Jesus, Annie, you're beginning to appal me. There's something scary about stupidity made coherent. I can deal

51

with idiots, and I can deal with sensible argument, but I don't know how to deal with you. Where's my cricket bat?

ANNIE: Your cricket bat?

HENRY: Yes. It's a new approach.

(*He heads out into the hall.*)

ANNIE: Are you trying to be funny?

HENRY: No, I'm serious.

(*He goes out while she watches in wary disbelief. He returns with an old cricket bat.*)

ANNIE: You better not be.

HENRY: Right, you silly cow—

ANNIE: Don't you bloody dare—

HENRY: Shut up and listen. This thing here, which looks like a wooden club, is actually several pieces of particular wood cunningly put together in a certain way so that the whole thing is sprung, like a dance floor. It's for hitting cricket balls with. If you get it right, the cricket ball will travel two hundred yards in four seconds, and all you've done is give it a knock like knocking the top off a bottle of stout, and it makes a noise like a trout taking a fly . . . (*He clucks his tongue to make the noise.*) What we're trying to do is to write cricket bats, so that when we throw up an idea and give it a little knock, it might . . . *travel* . . . (*He clucks his tongue again and picks up the script.*) Now, what we've got here is a lump of wood of roughly the same shape trying to be a cricket bat, and if you hit a ball with it, the ball will travel about ten feet and you will drop the bat and dance about shouting 'Ouch!' with your hands stuck into your armpits. (*Indicating the cricket bat.*) This isn't better because someone says it's better, or because there's a conspiracy by the MCC to keep cudgels out of Lords. It's better because it's better. You don't believe me, so I suggest you go out to bat with this and see how you get on. 'You're a strange boy, Billy, how old are you?' 'Twenty, but I've lived more than you'll ever live.' Ooh, ouch!

(*He drops the script and hops about with his hands in his armpits, going 'Ouch!'* ANNIE *watches him expressionlessly until he desists.*)

ANNIE: I hate you.

HENRY: I love you. I'm your pal. I'm your best mate. I look after you. You're the only chap.

ANNIE: Oh, Hen . . . Can't you help?

HENRY: What did you expect me to do?

ANNIE: Well . . . cut it and shape it . . .

HENRY: Cut it and shape it. Henry of Mayfair. Look—he can't write. I would have to write it for him.

ANNIE: Well, write it for him.

HENRY: I can't.

ANNIE: Why?

HENRY: Because it's *balls*. Mary's part is the least of it—it's merely ham-fisted. But when he gets into his stride, or rather his lurch, announcing every stale revelation of the newly enlightened, like stout Cortez coming upon the Pacific—war is profits, politicians are puppets, Parliament is a farce, justice is a fraud, property is theft . . . It's all here: the Stock Exchange, the arms dealers, the press barons . . . You can't fool Brodie—patriotism is propaganda, religion is a con trick, royalty is an anachronism . . . Pages and pages of it. It's like being run over very slowly by a travelling freak show of favourite simpletons, the india rubber pedagogue, the midget intellectual, the human panacea . . .

ANNIE: It's his view of the world. Perhaps from where he's standing you'd see it the same way.

HENRY: Or perhaps I'd realize where I'm standing. Or at least that I'm standing *somewhere*. There is, I suppose, a world of objects which have a certain form, like this coffee mug. I turn it, and it has no handle. I tilt it, and it has no cavity. But there is something real here which is always a mug with a handle. I suppose. But politics, justice, patriotism—they aren't even like coffee mugs. There's nothing real there separate from our perception of them. So if you try to change them as though there were something there to change, you'll get frustrated, and frustration will finally make you violent. If you know this and proceed with humility, you may perhaps alter people's perceptions so that they behave a little differently at that axis of behaviour

53

where we locate politics or justice; but if you don't know this, then you're acting on a mistake. Prejudice is the expression of this mistake.

ANNIE: Or such is your perception.

HENRY: All right.

ANNIE: And who wrote it, why he wrote it, *where* he wrote it—none of these things count with you?

HENRY: Leave me out of it. They don't count. Maybe Brodie got a raw deal, maybe he didn't. I don't know. It doesn't count. He's a lout with language. I can't help somebody who thinks, or thinks he thinks, that editing a newspaper is censorship, or that throwing bricks is a demonstration while building tower blocks is social violence, or that unpalatable statement is provocation while disrupting the speaker is the exercise of free speech . . . Words don't deserve that kind of malarkey. They're innocent, neutral, precise, standing for this, describing that, meaning the other, so if you look after them you can build bridges across incomprehension and chaos. But when they get their corners knocked off, they're no good any more, and Brodie knocks corners off without knowing he's doing it. So everything he builds is jerry-built. It's rubbish. An intelligent child could push it over. I don't think writers are sacred, but words are. They deserve respect. If you get the right ones in the right order, you can nudge the world a little or make a poem which children will speak for you when you're dead.

(ANNIE *goes to the typewriter, pulls out the page from the machine and reads it.*)

ANNIE: 'Seventy-nine. Interior. Commander's capsule. From Zadok's p.o.v. we see the green glow of the laser strike-force turning towards us. BCU Zadok's grim smile. *Zadok:* "I think it's going to work. Here they come!" *Kronk,* voice over: "Hold your course!" *Zadok:—*'

HENRY: (*Interrupts*) That's not words, that's pictures. The movies. Anyway, alimony doesn't count. If Charlotte made it legal with that architect she's shacked up with, I'd be writing the real stuff.

(ANNIE *lets the page drop on to the typewriter.*)

ANNIE: You never wrote mine.

HENRY: That's true. I didn't. I tried.

I can't remember when I last felt so depressed.

Oh yes. Yesterday.

Don't be rotten to me. I'll come to Glasgow and I'll sit in your dressing-room and I'll write Kronk and Zadok every night while you're doing *'Tis Pity She's a Whore*.

ANNIE: I'm not going to Glasgow.

HENRY: Yes, you bloody are.

ANNIE: No I'm bloody not. We'll get Brodie's play off the ground. I want to do it. *I* want to do it. Don't *I* count? Hen? (*Pause*) Well, I can see it's difficult for a man of your fastidious tastes. Let's have some literacy. Something decent. (ANNIE *stabs her finger on to the small radio on* HENRY's *desk. Quietly it starts playing pop. She starts to go out of the room.*)

HENRY: (*Exasperated*) *Why Brodie?* Do you fancy him or what? (*She looks back at him and he sees that he has made a mistake.*) I take it back.

ANNIE: Too late.

(*She leaves the room.*)

SCENE SIX

ANNIE *and* BILLY.

ANNIE *is sitting by the window of a moving train. She is immersed in a paperback book.*

BILLY *walks into view and pauses, looking at her for a moment. She is unaware of his presence. He carries a zipped grip bag. He speaks with a Scottish accent.*

BILLY: Excuse me, is this seat taken?

(ANNIE *hardly raises her eyes.*)

ANNIE: No.

(BILLY *sits down next to or opposite her. He puts the grip on the seat next to him. He looks at her. She doesn't look up from her book. He looks at his watch and then out of the*

55

window and then back at her.)

BILLY: You'd think with all these Fascists the trains would be on time.

(ANNIE *looks up at him and jumps a mile. She gives a little squeal.)*

ANNIE: Jesus, you gave me a shock.

(*She looks at him, pleased and amused.)*

You fool.

(BILLY *drops the accent.)*

BILLY: Hello.

ANNIE: I didn't know you were on the train.

BILLY: Yes, well, there you are. How are you?

ANNIE: All right. I gather you read it, then.

BILLY: Brodie's play? Yes, I read it.

ANNIE: And?

BILLY: He can't write.

(*Small pause.)*

ANNIE: I know.

I just thought it was something you'd do well.

BILLY: Oh, yes. I could do a job on it.

Are you going to do it?

ANNIE: I hope so. Not as it is, I suppose. Thank you for reading it anyway.

BILLY: Do you mind me coming to sit with you?

ANNIE: No, not at all.

BILLY: It doesn't mean we have to talk.

ANNIE: It's all right.

BILLY: How do you feel?

ANNIE: Scared. I'm always scared. I think, this is the one where I get found out.

BILLY: Well, better in Glasgow.

ANNIE: Is anyone else on this train?

BILLY: No, we're completely alone.

ANNIE: I mean any of *us*, the others.

BILLY: I don't know. Some of them are flying up, on the shuttle.

ANNIE: I fancied the train.

BILLY: I fancied it with you.

(ANNIE *meets his look.)*

ANNIE: Billy . . .

BILLY: What did you think when you saw me?

ANNIE: Just now?

BILLY: No. On the first day.

ANNIE: I thought God, he's so *young*.

BILLY: (*Scottish*) I've lived more than you'll ever live.

ANNIE: All right, all right.

BILLY: I'm the one who should be scared. You're smashing.

ANNIE: I don't feel right.

BILLY: You seem right to me.

ANNIE: I'm older than you.

BILLY: That doesn't matter.

ANNIE: I'm a lot older. I'm going to look more like your mother than your sister.

BILLY: That's all right, so long as it's incest. Anyway, I like older women.

ANNIE: Billy, you mustn't keep flirting with me.

BILLY: Why not?

ANNIE: Well, because there's no point. Will you stop?

BILLY: No. Is that all right?
    (*Pause*)

ANNIE: Did you know I was going to be on this train?

BILLY: (*Nods*) Watched you get on. I thought I'd come and find you when it got started.

ANNIE: You certainly thought about it.

BILLY: I had to wait until the inspector came round. I haven't got a first-class ticket.

ANNIE: What will you do if he comes back?

BILLY: I'll say you're my mum. How come you get a first-class ticket?

ANNIE: I don't really. I'm afraid I upped it myself.

BILLY: You approve of the class system?

ANNIE: You mean on trains or in general?

BILLY: In general. Travelling first-class.

ANNIE: There's no system. People group together when they've got something in common. Sometimes it's religion and sometimes it's, I don't know, breeding budgies or being at Eton. Big and small groups overlapping. You can't blame

them. It's a cultural thing; it's not *classes* or *system*.
(*She makes a connection.*)
There's nothing really *there*—it's just the way you see it.
Your perception.

BILLY: Bloody brilliant. There's people who've spent their lives trying to get rid of the class system, and you've done it without leaving your seat.

ANNIE: Well . . .

BILLY: The only problem with your argument is that you've got to be travelling first-class to really appreciate it.

ANNIE: I . . .

BILLY: Where do you get all that from? Did you just make it up? It's daft. I prefer Brodie. He sounds like rubbish, but you know he's right. You sound all right, but you know it's rubbish.

ANNIE: Why won't you do his play, then?

BILLY: I didn't say I wouldn't. I'll do it if you're doing it.

ANNIE: You shouldn't do it for the wrong reasons.

BILLY: Why not? Does he care?

ANNIE: You said he can't write.

BILLY: He can't write like your husband. But your husband's a first-class writer.

ANNIE: Are you being nasty about Henry?

BILLY: No. I saw *House of Cards*. I thought it was quite good.

ANNIE: He'll be relieved to hear that.
(*Pause*)

BILLY: Don't go off me.

ANNIE: If you weren't a child, you'd know that you won't get anywhere with a married woman if you're snotty about her husband. Remember that with the next one.

BILLY: I'faith, I mean no harm, sister. I'm just scared sick of you. How is't with ye?

ANNIE: I am very well, brother.

BILLY: Trust me, but I am sick; I fear so sick 'twill cost my life.

ANNIE: Mercy forbid it! 'Tis not so, I hope.

BILLY: I think you love me, sister.

ANNIE: Yes, you know I do.

BILLY: I know't, indeed. You're very fair.

ANNIE: Nay, then, I see you have a merry sickness.

BILLY: That's as it proves. The poets feign, I read,
That Juno for her forehead did exceed
All other goddesses; but I durst swear
Your forehead exceeds hers, as hers did theirs.

ANNIE: 'Troth, this is pretty!

BILLY: Such a pair of stars
As are thine eyes would, like Promethean fire,
If gently glanced, give life to senseless stones.

ANNIE: Fie upon ye!

BILLY: The lily and the rose, most sweetly strange,
Upon your dimpled cheeks do strive for change:
Such lips would tempt a saint; such hands as those
Would make an anchorite lascivious.

ANNIE: O, you are a trim youth!

BILLY: Herc!
(*His 'reading' has been getting less and less discreet. Now he stands up and opens his shirt.*)

ANNIE: (*Giggling*) Oh, leave off.
(*She looks around nervously.*)

BILLY: (*Starting to shout*) And here's my breast; strike home!
Rip up my bosom; there thou shalt behold
A heart in which is writ the truth I speak.

ANNIE: You daft idiot.

BILLY: Yes, most earnest. You cannot love?

ANNIE: Stop it.

BILLY: My tortured soul
Hath felt affliction in the heat of death.
Oh, Annabella, I am quite undone!

ANNIE: Billy!

SCENE SEVEN

HENRY *and* CHARLOTTE *and* DEBBIE.
The living-room of Scene 2, without all the records. CHARLOTTE *is searching through a file of newspaper cuttings and programmes. A large, loaded ruck-sack is sitting by the door.* DEBBIE *is smoking.*

HENRY: Since when did you smoke?

DEBBIE: I don't know. Years. At school. Me and Terry used to light up in the boiler room.

HENRY: *I* and Terry.

DEBBIE: I and Terry. Are you sure?

HENRY: It doesn't sound right but it's correct. I paid school fees so that you wouldn't be barred by your natural disabilities from being taught Latin and learning to speak English.

CHARLOTTE: I thought it was so that she'd be a virgin a bit longer.

HENRY: It was also so that she'd speak English. *Virgo syntacta.*

DEBBIE: You were done, Henry. Nobody left the boiler room virgo with Terry.

HENRY: I wish you'd stop celebrating your emancipation by flicking it at me like a wet towel. Did the staff know about this lout, Terry?

DEBBIE: He was on the staff. He taught Latin.

HENRY: Oh well, that's all right then.

CHARLOTTE: Apparently she'd already lost it riding anyway.

HENRY: That doesn't count.

CHARLOTTE: In the tackroom.

HENRY: God's truth. The groom.

CHARLOTTE: That's why he was bow-legged.

HENRY: I told you—I said you've got to warn her about being carried away.

DEBBIE: You don't get carried away in jodhpurs. It needs absolute determination.

HENRY: Will you stop this.

CHARLOTTE: No. I can't find it. It was yonks ago. I mean, not being catty, I was nearer the right age.

HENRY: Does it really matter who played Giovanni to your Annabella in *'Tis Pity She's a Whore*?

CHARLOTTE: I just think it's awful to have forgotten his name.

DEBBIE: Perhaps he's forgotten yours.

CHARLOTTE: But it was *my* virginity, not his.

DEBBIE: Was it actually on stage?

CHARLOTTE: Don't be silly—it was a British Council tour. No, it was in a boarding house in Zagreb.

60

DEBBIE: A bawdy house?

CHARLOTTE: The British Council has a lot to answer for.

HENRY: Look, we're supposed to be discussing a family crisis.

CHARLOTTE: What's that?

HENRY: Our daughter going on the streets.

DEBBIE: On the *road*, not the streets.

CHARLOTTE: Stop being so dramatic.

HENRY: I have a right to be dramatic.

CHARLOTTE: I see what you mean.

HENRY: I'm her father.

CHARLOTTE: Oh, I see what you mean.

HENRY: She's too young to go off with a man.

CHARLOTTE: She's certainly too young to go off without one. It's all right. He's nice.

(CHARLOTTE *has given up her search of the file and now leaves carrying the file.*)

(*To* DEBBIE.) If I'm in the bath when he comes I want to see you both before you disappear.

(CHARLOTTE *goes out.*)

HENRY: What does he play? (DEBBIE *looks blank.*) Ma said he's a musician.

DEBBIE: Oh—um—steam organ . . .

HENRY: A travelling steam organist? (*Pause*) He's not a musician.

DEBBIE: Fairground.

HENRY: Well, swings and roundabouts.

DEBBIE: Tunnel of love. How's Annie?

HENRY: In Glasgow.

DEBBIE: Don't worry, Henry, I'll be happy.

HENRY: Happy? What do you mean happy?

DEBBIE: Happy! Like a warm puppy.

HENRY: Dear Christ, is that what it's all come down to?—no philosophy that can't be printed on a T-shirt. You don't get visited by happiness like being lucky with the weather. The weather is the weather.

DEBBIE: And happiness?

HENRY: Happiness is . . . equilibrium. Shift your weight.

DEBBIE: Are you happy, Henry?

HENRY: I don't much like your calling me Henry. I liked being called Fa. Fa and Ma.

DEBBIE: Happy days, eh? How're the Everlys getting on? And the Searchers. How's old Elvis?

HENRY: He's dead.

DEBBIE: I did know that. I mean how's he holding up apart from that?

HENRY: I never went for him much. 'All Shook Up' was the last good one. However, I suppose that's the fate of all us artists.

DEBBIE: Death?

HENRY: People saying they preferred the early stuff.

DEBBIE: Well, maybe you were better then.

HENRY: Didn't you like the last one?

DEBBIE: What, *House of Cards*? Well, it wasn't about anything, except did she have it off or didn't she? What a crisis. Infidelity among the architect class. Again.

HENRY: It was about self-knowledge through pain.

DEBBIE: No, it was about did she have it off or didn't she. As if having it off is infidelity.

HENRY: Most people think it is.

DEBBIE: Most people think *not* having it off is *fidelity*. They think all relationships hinge in the middle. Sex or no sex. What a fantastic range of possibilities. Like an on/off switch. Did she or didn't she. By Henry Ibsen. Why would you want to make it such a crisis?

HENRY: I don't know, why would I?

DEBBIE: It's what comes of making such a mystery of it. When I was twelve I was obsessed. Everything was sex. Latin was sex. The dictionary fell open at *meretrix*, a harlot. You could feel the mystery coming off the word like musk. *Meretrix*! This was none of your *mensa*-a-table, this was a flash from the forbidden planet, and it was everywhere. History was sex, French was sex, art was sex, the Bible, poetry, penfriends, games, music, everything was sex except biology which was obviously sex but obviously not *really* sex, not the one which was secret and ecstatic and wicked and a sacrament and all the things it was supposed to be but couldn't be at one and the same time—I got that

62

in the boiler room and it turned out to be biology after all. That's what free love is free of—propaganda.

HENRY: Don't get too good at that.

DEBBIE: What?

HENRY: Persuasive nonsense. Sophistry in a phrase so neat you can't see the loose end that would unravel it. It's flawless but wrong. A perfect dud. You can do that with words, bless 'em. How about 'What free love is free of, is love'? Another little gem. You could put a 'what' on the end of it, like Bertie Wooster, 'What free love is free of is love, what?'—and the words would go on replicating themselves like a spiral of DNA . . . 'What love is free of love?—*free* love is what love, what?—'

DEBBIE: (*Interrupting*) *Fa*. You're going on.

HENRY: Yes. Well, I remember, the first time I succumbed to the sensation that the universe was dispensable minus one lady—

DEBBIE: Don't write it, Fa. Just say it. The first time you fell in love. What?

HENRY: It's to do with knowing and being known. I remember how it stopped seeming odd that in biblical Greek knowing was used for making love. Whosit knew so-and-so. Carnal knowledge. It's what lovers trust each other with. Knowledge of each other, not of the flesh but through the flesh, knowledge of self, the real him, the real her, *in extremis,* the mask slipped from the face. Every other version of oneself is on offer to the public. We share our vivacity, grief, sulks, anger, joy . . . we hand it out to anybody who happens to be standing around, to friends and family with a momentary sense of indecency perhaps, to strangers without hesitation. Our lovers share us with the passing trade. But in pairs we insist that we give ourselves to each other. What selves? What's left? What else is there that hasn't been dealt out like a deck of cards? A sort of knowledge. Personal, final, uncompromised. Knowing, being known. I revere that. Having that is being rich, you can be generous about what's shared—she walks, she talks, she laughs, she lends a sympathetic ear, she kicks off her

63

shoes and dances on the tables, she's everybody's and it don't mean a thing, let them eat cake; knowledge is something else, the undealt card, and while it's held it makes you free-and-easy and nice to know, and when it's gone everything is pain. Every single thing. Every object that meets the eye, a pencil, a tangerine, a travel poster. As if the physical world has been wired up to pass a current back to the part of your brain where imagination glows like a filament in a lobe no bigger than a torch bulb. Pain.
(*Pause*)

DEBBIE: Has Annie got someone else then?

HENRY: Not as far as I know, thank you for asking.

DEBBIE: Apologies.

HENRY: Don't worry.

DEBBIE: Don't you. Exclusive rights isn't love, it's colonization.

HENRY: Christ almighty. Another *ersatz* masterpiece. Like Michelangelo working in polystyrene.

DEBBIE: Do you know what your problem is, Henry?

HENRY: What?

DEBBIE: Your Latin mistress never took you into the boiler room.

HENRY: Well, at least I passed.

DEBBIE: Only in Latin.
(*Doorbell*)
Do me a favour.

HENRY: What?

DEBBIE: Stay here.

HENRY: That bad, is he?

DEBBIE: He's frightened of you.

HENRY: Jesus.
(CHARLOTTE *enters in a bath robe, a towel round her hair perhaps. She carries a bunch of postcards.*)

CHARLOTTE: Ten postcards—stamped and addressed. Every week I get a postcard you get ten quid. No postcards, no remittance.
(*She gives* DEBBIE *the postcards.*)

DEBBIE: Oh—Charley—(*kisses* CHARLOTTE).
See you, Henry.

HENRY: There; my blessing with thee. And these few precepts

64

in thy memory . . .

DEBBIE: Too late, Fa. Love you. (*Kisses him.*)

(DEBBIE *leaves with the ruck-sack followed by* CHARLOTTE.
HENRY *waits until* CHARLOTTE *returns.*)

CHARLOTTE: What a good job we sold the pony.

HENRY: Musician is he? She's hardly seventeen.

CHARLOTTE: Almost over the hill for an Elizabethan heroine.
(*Pause*) How's Annie? Are you going to Glasgow for the
first night?

HENRY: They don't open for a couple of weeks.

CHARLOTTE: Who's playing Giovanni?

HENRY: I don't know.

CHARLOTTE: Aren't you interested?

HENRY: Should I be?

CHARLOTTE: There's something touching about you, Henry.
Everybody should be like you. Not interested. It used to
bother me that you were never bothered. Even when I got
talked into that dreadful nudie film because it was in
Italian and Italian films were supposed to be art . . . God,
that dates me, doesn't it? Debbie's into Australian films.
Australian. Not Chips Rafferty—actual *films.*

HENRY: You've gone off again.

CHARLOTTE: Yes, well, it didn't bother you so I decided it
meant you were having it off right left and centre and it
wasn't supposed to matter. By the time I realized you were
the last romantic it was too late. I found it *didn't* matter.

HENRY: Well, now that it doesn't . . . How many—um—
roughly how many—?

CHARLOTTE: Nine.

(*Pause*)

HENRY: Gosh.

CHARLOTTE: And look what your one did compared to my nine.

HENRY: Nine?

CHARLOTTE: Feel betrayed?

HENRY: Surprised. I thought we'd made a commitment.

CHARLOTTE: There are no commitments, only bargains. And
they have to be made again every day. You think making a
commitment is *it*. Finish. You think it sets like a concrete

65

platform and it'll take any strain you want to put on it.
You're committed. You don't have to prove anything. In
fact you can afford a little neglect, indulge in a little bit of
sarcasm here and there, isolate yourself when you want to.
Underneath it's concrete for life. I'm a cow in some ways,
but you're an idiot. *Were* an idiot.

HENRY: Better luck next time.

CHARLOTTE: You too.

Have a drink?

HENRY: I don't think so, thank you.

How are things with your friend? An architect, isn't he?

CHARLOTTE: I had to give him the elbow. Well, he sort of left.

I called him the architect of my misfortune.

HENRY: What was the matter with him?

CHARLOTTE: Very possessive type. I came home from a job, I'd
been away only a couple of days, and he said, why did I
take my diaphragm? He'd been through my bathroom
cabinet, would you believe? And then, not finding it, he
went through everything else. Can't have that.

HENRY: What did you say?

CHARLOTTE: I said, I didn't *take* my diaphragm, it just went
with me. So he said, what about the tube of Duragel?
I must admit he had me there.

HENRY: You should have said, 'Duragel!—no wonder the
bristles fell out of my toothbrush.'

CHARLOTTE: (*Laughs*) Cheers.

HENRY: (*Toasting with an empty hand*) Cheers.

(HENRY *stands up*.)

CHARLOTTE: Do you have to go?

HENRY: Yes, I ought to.

CHARLOTTE: You don't fancy one for the road?

HENRY: No, really.

CHARLOTTE: Or a drink?

HENRY: (*Smiles*) No offence.

CHARLOTTE: Remember what I said.

HENRY: What was that? (*Pause*) Oh . . . yes. No commitments.
Only bargains. The trouble is I don't really believe it. I'd
rather be an idiot. It's a kind of idiocy I like. 'I use you

because you love me. I love you so use me. Be indulgent,
negligent, preoccupied, premenstrual . . . your credit is
infinite, I'm yours, I'm committed . . .
It's no trick loving somebody at their *best*. Love is loving
them at their worst. Is that romantic? Well, good.
Everything should be romantic. Love, work, music,
literature, virginity, loss of virginity . . .

CHARLOTTE: You've still got one to lose, Henry.

SCENE EIGHT*

ANNIE *and* BILLY.

An empty space.
They are kissing, embracing: wearing rehearsal clothes.

BILLY: Come, Annabella,—no more sister now,
  But love, a name more gracious,—do not blush,
  Beauty's sweet wonder, but be proud to know
  That yielding thou hast conquered, and inflamed
  A heart whose tribute is thy brother's life.

ANNIE: And mine is his. O, how these stol'n contents
  Would print a modest crimson on my cheeks,
  Had any but my heart's delight prevailed!

BILLY: I marvel why the chaster of your sex
  Should think this pretty toy called maidenhead
  So strange a loss, when, being lost, 'tis nothing,
  And you are still the same.

ANNIE: 'Tis well for you;
  Now you can talk.

BILLY: Music as well consists
  In the ear as in the playing.

ANNIE: O, you're wanton!
  Tell on't you're best; do.

BILLY: Thou wilt chide me, then.

* In order to accommodate a scene change, Scene 8 was spoken twice,
once as a 'word rehearsal' and then again as an 'acting rehearsal'.

Kiss me:—
   (*He kisses her lightly.*)
ANNIE: (*Quietly*) Billy . . .
   (*She returns the kiss in earnest.*)

SCENE NINE

HENRY *and* ANNIE.

The living-room. HENRY *is alone, sitting in a chair, doing nothing.*
It's like the beginning of Scene 1 and Scene 3.
ANNIE *is heard letting herself in through the front door. Then she comes*
in from the hall.
ANNIE *enters wearing a topcoat and carrying a suitcase and a small*
travelling bag.

ANNIE: Hello, I'm back.
   (*She puts down the suitcase and the bag and goes to kiss*
   HENRY.)
HENRY: Hello.
   (*She starts taking off her coat.*)
   How was it?
ANNIE: We had a good finish—a woman in the audience was
   sick. Billy came on with my heart skewered on his dagger
   and—ugh—whoops!
   (*She takes her coat out into the hall, reappears and goes to the*
   travelling bag.)
HENRY: I thought you were coming back overnight.
   (*From the travelling bag* ANNIE *takes a small, smart-looking*
   carrier bag with handles, a purchase from a boutique.)
ANNIE: What have you been doing? How's the film?
   (*She gives the present to* HENRY, *kissing him lightly.*)
HENRY: I thought you were on the sleeper.
ANNIE: What's the matter?
HENRY: I was wondering what happened to you.
ANNIE: Nothing happened to me. Have you had lunch?
HENRY: No. Did you catch the early train this morning, then?

ANNIE: Yes. Scratch lunch, all right?
  (*She goes into the kitchen and returns after a moment.*)
  My God, it's all gone downhill since Sunday. Hasn't Mrs
  Chamberlain been?
HENRY: I phoned the hotel.
ANNIE: When?
HENRY: Last night. They said you'd checked out.
ANNIE: Did they?
  (*She picks up her suitcase and goes out into the bedroom.*
  HENRY *doesn't move. A few moments later* ANNIE *reappears,
  without the suitcase and almost walking backwards.*)
  Oh, God, Hen. Have we had burglars? What were you
  doing?
HENRY: Where were you?
ANNIE: On the sleeper. I don't know why I said I came down
  this morning. It just seemed easier. I wasn't there last night
  because I caught the train straight from the theatre.
HENRY: Was the train late arriving?
ANNIE: Do you want to see my ticket?
HENRY: Well, have you been to the zoo?
  (*She meets his look expressionlessly.*)
  Who were you with?
ANNIE: Don't be like this, Hen. You're not like this.
HENRY: Yes, I am.
ANNIE: I don't want you to. It's humiliating.
HENRY: I really am not trying to humiliate you.
ANNIE: For you, I mean. It's humiliating for you. (*Pause*) I
  travelled down with one of the company. We had breakfast
  at Euston. He was waiting for a train. I stayed talking.
  Then I came home, not thinking that suddenly after two
  and a half years I'd be asked to account for my movements.
HENRY: You got off the sleeper and spent the morning sitting at
  Euston?
ANNIE: Yes.
HENRY: You and this actor.
ANNIE: Yes. Can I go now?
  (*She turns away.*)
HENRY: How did you sleep?

(*She turns to look at him blankly.*)

Well, did you?

ANNIE: Did I what?

What's the point? You'd only wonder if I was lying.

HENRY: Would you lie?

ANNIE: I might.

HENRY: Did you?

ANNIE: No. You see? I'm going to tidy up and put everything back.

HENRY: Do you want to know what I was looking for?

ANNIE: No.

(*She turns towards the bedroom.*)

HENRY: Was it Billy?

(*She turns back.*)

ANNIE: Why Billy?

HENRY: I know it's him. Billy, Billy, Billy, the name keeps dropping, each time without significance, but it can't help itself. Hapless as a secret in a computer. Blip, blip. Billy, Billy. Talk to me.

I'm sorry about the bedroom.

ANNIE: You should have put everything back. Everything would be the way it was.

HENRY: You can't put things back. They won't go back. Talk to me.

I'm your chap. I know about this. We start off like one of those caterpillars designed for a particular leaf. The exclusive voracity of love. And then not. How strange that the way of things is not suspended to meet our special case. But it never is. I don't want anyone else but sometimes, surprisingly, there's someone, not the prettiest or the most available, but you know that in another life it would be her. Or him, don't you find? A small quickening. The room responds slightly to being entered. Like a raised blind. Nothing intended, and a long way from doing anything, but you catch the glint of being someone else's possibility, and it's a sort of politeness to show you haven't missed it, so you push it a little, well within safety, but there's that sense of a promise almost being made in the touching and kissing

70

without which no one can seem to say good morning in this poncy business and one more push would do it. Billy. Right?

ANNIE: Yes.

HENRY: I love you.

ANNIE: And I you. I wouldn't be here if I didn't.

HENRY: Tell me, then.

ANNIE: I love you.

HENRY: Not that.

ANNIE: Yes, that. That's all I'd need to know.

HENRY: You'd need more.

ANNIE: No.

HENRY: I need it. I can manage knowing if you did but I can't manage not knowing if you did or not. I won't be able to work.

ANNIE: Don't blackmail.

HENRY: You'd ask me.

ANNIE: I never have.

HENRY: There's never *been* anything.

ANNIE: Dozens. For the first year at least, every halfway decent looking woman under fifty you were ever going to meet.

HENRY: But you learned better.

ANNIE: No, I just learned not to care. There was nothing to keep you here so I assumed you wanted to stay. I stopped caring about the rest of it.

HENRY: I care. Tell me.

ANNIE: (*Hardening*) I did tell you. I spent the morning talking to Billy in a station cafeteria instead of coming straight home to you and I fibbed about the train because *that* seemed like infidelity—but all you want to know is did I sleep with him first?

HENRY: Yes. Did you?

ANNIE: No.

HENRY: Did you want to?

ANNIE: Oh, for God's sake!

HENRY: You can ask me.

ANNIE: I prefer to respect your privacy.

HENRY: I have none. I disclaim it. Did you?

71

ANNIE: What about your dignity, then?

HENRY: Yes, you'd behave better than me. I don't believe in behaving well. I don't believe in debonair relationships. 'How's your lover today, Amanda?' 'In the pink, Charles. How's yours?' I believe in mess, tears, pain, self-abasement, loss of self-respect, nakedness. Not caring doesn't seem much different from not loving. Did you? You did, didn't you?

ANNIE: This isn't caring. If I had an affair, it would be out of need. Care about that. You won't play on my guilt or my remorse. I'd have none.

HENRY: Need?
What did you talk about?

ANNIE: Brodie mostly.

HENRY: Yes. I had it coming.

ANNIE: Billy wants to do Brodie's play.

HENRY: When are you going to see Billy again?

ANNIE: He's going straight into another show. I promised to see him. I want to see him.

HENRY: Fine, when should we go? It's all right to come with you, is it?

ANNIE: Why not? Don't let me out of your sight, eh, Hen?

HENRY: When were you thinking of going?

ANNIE: I thought the weekend.

HENRY: And where is it?

ANNIE: Well, Glasgow.

HENRY: Billy travelled down with you from Glasgow and then took a train back?

ANNIE: Yes.

HENRY: And I'm supposed to score points for dignity. I don't think I can. It'll become my only thought. It'll replace thinking.

ANNIE: You mustn't do that. You have to find a part of yourself where I'm not important or you won't be worth loving. It's awful what you did to my clothes and everything. I mean what you did to yourself. It's not you. And it's you I love.

HENRY: Actually I don't think I can manage the weekend. I hope it goes well.

72

ANNIE: Thank you. (*She moves towards the bedroom.*)
HENRY: What does Billy think of Brodie's play?
ANNIE: He says he can't write.

> (*She leaves.* HENRY *takes his present out of its bag. It is a tartan scarf.*)

SCENE TEN

BILLY *and* ANNIE.

ANNIE *sits reading on the train.*
BILLY *approaches the seat next to* ANNIE. *He speaks with a Scottish accent. He carries a grip.*
The dialogue is amplified through a mike.

BILLY: Excuse me, is this seat taken?
ANNIE: No.
BILLY: Mind if I sit down?
ANNIE: It's a free country.

> (BILLY *sits down.*)

BILLY: D'you reckon?
ANNIE: Sorry?
BILLY: You reckon it's a free country?

> (ANNIE *ignores him.*)
> Going far?

ANNIE: To London.
BILLY: All the way.

> (ANNIE *starts to move to an empty seat.*)
> I'll let you read.

ANNIE: Thank you.

> (*She sits in the empty seat.*)

BILLY: My name's Bill.

> (*She ignores him.*)
> Can I just ask you one question?

ANNIE: Mary.
BILLY: Can I just ask you one question, Mary?
ANNIE: One.

BILLY: Do you know what time this train is due to arrive in
    London?

ANNIE: At about half-past one, I believe, if it's on time.

BILLY: You put me in mind of Mussolini, Mary. People used to
    say about Mussolini, he may be a Fascist, but—

ANNIE: No—that's wrong—that's the old script—

BILLY: (*Swears under his breath.*) Sorry, Roger . . .

ROGER: (*Voice off*) Okay, cut the tape.

ANNIE: From the top, Roger?

ROGER: (*Voice off*) Give us a minute.

> (*A light change reveals that the setting is a fake, in a TV
> studio.* ANNIE *gets up and moves away.* BILLY *joins her. They
> exchange a few words, and she moves back to her seat, leaving
> him estranged, an unhappy feeling between them.*
> *After a moment the scene fades out.*)

SCENE ELEVEN

HENRY *and* ANNIE.

HENRY *is alone listening to the radio, which is playing Bach's Air on a
G String.*

ANNIE *enters from the bedroom, dressed to go out, and she is in a hurry.*

HENRY: (*Urgently, on seeing her*) Listen—

ANNIE: I can't. I'm going to be late now.

HENRY: It's important. *Listen.*

ANNIE: What?

HENRY: *Listen.*

> (*She realizes that he means the radio. She listens for a few
> moments.*)
> What is it?

ANNIE: (*Pleased*) Do you like it?

HENRY: I *love* it.

ANNIE: (*Congratulating him*) It's Bach.

HENRY: The cheeky beggar.

ANNIE: What?

HENRY: He's stolen it.

ANNIE: *Bach?*

HENRY: Note for note. Practically a straight lift from Procul
　　Harum. And he can't even get it right. Hang on. I'll play
　　you the original.
　　(*He moves to get the record. She, pleased by him but going,*
　　moves to him.)

ANNIE: Work well.
　　(*She kisses him quickly and lightly but he forces the kiss into a*
　　less casual one. His voice, however, keeps its detachment.)

HENRY: You too.

ANNIE: Last day. Why don't you come?
　　(HENRY *shrugs.*)
　　No, all right.

HENRY: I'm only the ghost writer anyway.
　　(*The phone rings.*)

ANNIE: If that's them, say I've left.

HENRY: (*Into the phone*) She's left . . . Oh . . .
　　(*To* ANNIE.) It's your friend.
　　(*She hesitates.*)
　　Just go.
　　(ANNIE *takes the phone.*)

ANNIE: (*Into phone*) Billy . . .? Yes—what?—yes, of course—
　　I'm just late—yes—goodbye—all right . . . Yes, fine.
　　(*She hangs up.*) I love you. Do you understand?

HENRY: No.

ANNIE: Do you think it's unfair?

HENRY: No. It's as though I've been careless, left a door open
　　somewhere while preoccupied.

ANNIE: I'll stop.

HENRY: Not for me. I won't be the person who stopped you. I
　　can't be that. When I got upset you said you'd stop so I
　　try not to get upset. I don't get pathetic because when I got
　　pathetic I could feel how tedious it was, how unattractive.
　　Like Max, your ex. Remember Max? Love me because I'm
　　in pain. No good. Not in very good taste.
　　So.
　　Dignified cuckoldry is a difficult trick, but it can be done.

Think of it as modern marriage. We have got beyond hypocrisy, you and I. Exclusive rights isn't love, it's colonization.

ANNIE: Stop it—please stop it.

(*Pause*)

HENRY: The trouble is, I can't *find* a part of myself where you're not important. I write in order to be worth your while and to finance the way I want to live with you. Not the way *you* want to live. The way *I* want to live with *you*. Without you I wouldn't care. I'd eat tinned spaghetti and put on yesterday's clothes. But as it is I change my socks, and make money, and tart up Brodie's unspeakable drivel into speakable drivel so he can be an author too, like me. Not that it seems to have done him much good. Perhaps the authorities saw that it was a touch meretricious. *Meretrix, meretricis.* Harlot.

ANNIE: You shouldn't have done it if you didn't think it was right.

HENRY: You think it's right. I can't cope with more than one moral system at a time. Mine is that what you think is right is right. What you do is right. What you want is right. There was a tribe, wasn't there, which worshipped Charlie Chaplin. It worked just as well as any other theology, apparently. They loved Charlie Chaplin. I love you.

ANNIE: So you'll forgive me anything, is that it, Hen? I'm a selfish cow but you love me so you'll overlook it, is that right? Thank you, but that's not it. I wish I felt selfish, everything would be easy. Goodbye Billy. I don't need him. How can I need someone I spend half my time telling to grow up? I'm . . .—what's a petard?, I've often wondered.

HENRY: What?

ANNIE: A petard. Something you hoist, is it, piece of rope?

HENRY: I don't think so.

ANNIE: Well, anyway. All right?

HENRY: All right what? I keep marrying people who suddenly lose a wheel.

ANNIE: I don't feel selfish, I feel hoist. I send out waves, you know. Not free. Not interested. He sort of got in under the

76

radar. Acting daft on a train. Next thing I'm looking round for him, makes the day feel better, it's like love or something: no—love, absolutely, how can I say it wasn't? You weren't replaced, or even replaceable. But I liked it, being older for once, in charge, my pupil. And it was a long way north. And so on. I'm sorry I hurt you. But I meant it. It meant something. And now that it means less than I thought and I feel silly, I won't drop him as if it was nothing, a pick-up, it wasn't that, I'm not that. I just want him to stop needing me so I can stop behaving well. This is me behaving well. I have to choose who I hurt and I choose you because I'm yours. (*Pause. The phone rings.*) Maybe it's just me.

HENRY: (*Into phone*) Roger—? She's left, about ten minutes ago —yes, I know, dear, but—don't talk to me about unprofessional, Roger—you lost half a day shooting the war memorial with a boom shadow all over it—okay, scream at me if it makes you feel better—

(ANNIE *takes the phone out of his hand.*)

ANNIE: (*Into phone*) Keep your knickers on, it's only a bloody play.

(*She hangs up and starts to go.*)

(*Going*) Bye.

HENRY: Annie. (*Pause*) Yes, all right.

ANNIE: I need you.

HENRY: Yes, I know.

ANNIE: Please don't let it wear away what you feel for me. It won't, will it?

HENRY: No, not like that. It will go on or it will flip into its opposite.

What time will you be back?

ANNIE: Not late.

(*He nods at her. She nods back and leaves.* HENRY *sits down in his chair. Then he gets up and starts the record playing— Procul Harum's 'A Whiter Shade of Pale', which is indeed a version of Air on a G String.*

He stands listening to it, smiling at its Bach, until the vocals start. Then the smile gets overtaken.)

HENRY: Oh, please, please, please, please, *don't*.
(*Then blackout, but the music continues.*)

SCENE TWELVE

HENRY, ANNIE *and* BRODIE.
In the blackout the music gives way to recorded dialogue between
ANNIE *and* BILLY, *who speaks with a Scottish accent.*

BILLY: (*Voice*) Wait for me.

ANNIE: (*Voice*) Yes, I will.

BILLY: (*Voice*) Everything's got to change. Except you. Don't you
change.

ANNIE: (*Voice*) No. I won't. I'll wait for you and for everything
to change.

BILLY: (*Voice*) That could take longer. (*Laughs*) I might have to
do it myself.
(*By this time, light has appeared starting with the faint glow
from the television screen.*
BRODIE, *alone in the living-room, is twenty-five, wearing a
cheap suit. He is holding a tumbler of neat scotch, his attention
engaged by the television set and particularly by the
accompanying video machine. From the television the dialogue
has been followed by the echoing clang of a cell door, footsteps,
credit music . . .* BRODIE *turns the volume down.*
HENRY *enters from the kitchen carrying a small jug of water for*
BRODIE's *scotch. In the room there is wine for* HENRY *and
another glass for* ANNIE.
BRODIE *speaks with a Scottish accent.*)

BRODIE: Very handy, these machines. When did they come out?

HENRY: Well, I suppose they were coming out about the time
you were going in.

BRODIE: You can set them two weeks ahead.

HENRY: Yes.

BRODIE: How much?

HENRY: A few hundred. They vary.

78

BRODIE: I'll have to pinch one sometime.

HENRY: If you leave it a bit, they'll probably improve them so that you can have it recording concurrently with your sentence.

(BRODIE *looks at* HENRY *without expression.*)

BRODIE: Annie looked nice. She's come on a bit since *Rosie of the Royal Infirmary.* A good-looking woman.

(HENRY *doesn't answer.* ANNIE *enters from the kitchen with a dip, peanuts, etc. on a tray. She puts the tray down.* HENRY *pours wine into a third glass.*)

Just saying you looked nice.

ANNIE: Oh, yes?

BRODIE: The pretty one was supposed to be me, was he?

ANNIE: Well . . .

BRODIE: He's not a pansy, is he?

ANNIE: I don't think so.

(HENRY *hands her the glass of wine.*)

Thank you.

HENRY: (*To* BRODIE, *indicating the TV*) What did you think?

BRODIE: I liked it better before. You don't mind me saying?

HENRY: No.

ANNIE: It did work.

BRODIE: You mean getting me sprung?

ANNIE: No, I didn't mean that.

BRODIE: That's right. I got sprung by the militarists.

HENRY: I don't think I follow that.

BRODIE: Half a billion pounds for defence, nothing left for prisons. So you get three, four to a cell. First off, they tell the magistrates, for God's sake go easy, *fine* the bastards. But still they keep coming—four, five to a cell. Now they're frightened it's going to blow up. Even the warders are going on strike. So: 'Give us the money to build more prisons!' 'Can't be done, laddie, we're spending the money to keep the world free, not in prison.' So they start freeing the prisoners. Get it? I'm out because the missiles I was marching against are using up the money they need for a prison to put me in. Beautiful. Can I have another?

(*He holds up his empty glass for* ANNIE. *Slight pause.* HENRY

79

stays still.)

ANNIE: Please help yourself.

(BRODIE *does so.*)

BRODIE: Early release. There was eight of us just on my corridor. (*To* HENRY.) Not one of them a controversial TV author. I don't owe you.

HENRY: Is it against your principles to say thank you for *anything*, even a drink?

BRODIE: Fair enough. You had a go. You did your best. It probably needed something, to work in with their prejudices.

HENRY: Yes, they are a bit prejudiced, these drama producers. They don't like plays which go 'clunk' every time someone opens his mouth. They gang up against soap-box bigots with no idea that everything has a length. They think TV is a visual medium. (*To* ANNIE, *puzzled.*) Is this *him*?

BRODIE: Don't be clever with me, Henry, like you were clever with my play. I lived it and put my guts into it, and you came along and wrote it clever. Not for me. For her. I'm not stupid.

ANNIE: (*To* HENRY.) No, this isn't him.

BRODIE: Yes, it bloody is. That was me on the train, and this is me again, and I don't think you're that different either.

ANNIE: And *that* wasn't him. (*She points at the TV.*) He was helpless, like a three-legged calf, nervous as anything. A boy on the train. Chatting me up. Nice. He'd been in some trouble at the camp, some row, I forget, he was going absent without leave. He didn't know anything about a march. He didn't know anything about anything, except *Rosie of the Royal Infirmary*. By the time we got to London he would have followed me into the Ku Klux Klan. He tagged on. And when we were passing the war memorial he got his lighter out. It was one of those big chrome Zippos— click, snap. Private Brodie goes over the top to the slaughter, not an idea in his head except to impress me. What else could I do? He was my recruit.

HENRY: You should have told me. That one I would have known how to write.

ANNIE: Yes.

BRODIE: Listen—I'm still here.

ANNIE: So you are, Bill. Finish your drink, will you?

BRODIE: Why not?

(BRODIE *finishes his drink and stands up.*)

I can come back for some dip another time.

ANNIE: No time like the present.

(ANNIE *picks up the bowl of dip and smashes it into his face. She goes to the hall door, leaving it open while she briefly disappears to get* BRODIE'S *coat.*

HENRY *has stood up, but* BRODIE *isn't going to do anything. He carefully wipes his face with his handkerchief.*)

HENRY: Well, it was so interesting to meet you. I'd heard so much about you.

BRODIE: I don't really blame you, Henry. The price was right. I remember the time she came to visit me. She was in a blue dress, and there was a thrill coming off her like she was back on the box, but there was no way in. It was the first time I felt I was in prison. You know what I mean.

(ANNIE *stands at the door holding* BRODIE'S *coat. He takes it from her, ignoring her as he walks out. She follows him, and the front door is heard closing.* ANNIE *returns.*)

HENRY: I don't know what it did to him, but it scared the hell out of me. Are you all right?

(*She nods.*)

ANNIE: Are you all right?

(*The phone rings.* HENRY *picks it up.*)

HENRY: Hello.

(*Into the phone, suddenly uncomfortable.*) Oh, hello. Did you want to speak to Annie?

ANNIE: No.

HENRY: (*Suddenly relaxes*) Well, that's fantastic, Max!

(*To* ANNIE.) It's your ex. He's getting married.

(*To phone*) Congratulations. Who is she?

(HENRY *ferries this over to* ANNIE *with an expressive look, which she returns.* ANNIE *moves to* HENRY *and embraces his shoulders from behind. She leans on him tiredly while he deals with the phone.*)

Oh, I think you're very wise. To marry one actress is

unfortunate, to marry two is simply asking for it.

(ANNIE *kisses him. He covers the mouthpiece with his hand.*)

(*Into phone*) Really? Across a crowded room, eh?

ANNIE: I've had it. Look after me.

(*He covers the mouthpiece.*)

HENRY: Don't worry. I'm your chap.

(*Into phone*) Well, it's very decent of you to say so, Max.

(*To* ANNIE.) 'No hard feelings?' What does he mean? If it wasn't for me, he wouldn't be engaged *now*.

(ANNIE *disengages herself from him with a smile and goes around turning out the lights until the only light is coming from the bedroom door.*)

(*Into phone*) No. I'm afraid she isn't . . . She'll be so upset when I tell her . . . No, I mean when I tell her she missed you . . . No, she'll be delighted. I'm delighted, Max. Isn't love wonderful?

(ANNIE *finishes with the lights and goes out into the bedroom.* HENRY *is being impatiently patient with* MAX *on the phone, trying to end it.*)

HENRY: Yes, well, we look forward to meeting her. What? Oh, yes?

(*Absently he clicks on the little radio, which starts playing, softly, 'I'm a Believer' by the Monkees. He is immediately beguiled. He forgets* MAX *until the phone crackle gets back through to him.*)

Sorry. Yes, I'm still here.

(*He turns the song up slightly.*)